D1587130

WORLD CUP ARGENTINA

Introduction by
RON GREENWOOD
Written by
COLIN MALAM

Collins
Glasgow & London

DESIGN

ADS Graphics Unit Edinburgh

Art Director/Designer COLIN MARR
assisted by NEIL HAMILTON

Co-ordination and planning COLIN MARR and PAT O'BRIEN

PHOTOGRAPHS

ROGER PARKER   print production BOB THOMAS·

Cover and pages 4 (top and middle), 8–9, 12–15, 18–21, 28–9, 30–1, 33, 34, 37, 40–1 (and bottom inset), 51, 52–69, 71, 72–3, 77, 80–1 (top, inset and bottom), 82–3, 99, 101 (inset), 108, 109 (1, 2, 3, 5, 8, 9), 112 (12, 13, 14, 15, 16), 115, 116, 117 (bottom left), 120–1 (all bottom row), 122, 128

FRANK SPOONER PICTURES (GAMMA), London

Title page and pages 4 (bottom), 7, 9 (top and insets), 10, 16–17, 22–7, 35–6, 38–9, 40 (top inset), 44–5, 46–50, 79, 81 (black and white), 86, 90–1, 93, 94–5, 109 (4, 6, 7, 10, 11), 113, 117 (top, middle, inset and bottom left), 120–1 (middle and top insets), 125.

Picture editing   COLIN MARR

ACKNOWLEDGEMENTS

The author and publishers gratefully acknowledge the help of many people in producing this book, in particular, Jack Rollin, Norman Fox, Chris Davies, Carlos Fletcher, Claudia Bruscat and The Football Association and Scottish Football Association.

PRINTING

First published 1978
Copyright © Colin Malam 1978

Text set in 12 point Plantin
by Typesetting Services Glasgow.

Headings, datelines, panels and captions set in 30 and 18 point Stymie bold, 10 and 12 point Gill bold and 9 point Cheltenham Old Style by Artwork Associates, Edinburgh.

Colour separation by Gilchrist Bros. Leeds.

Printed and bound in Britain by
William Collins Sons & Co. Ltd. Glasgow.

CONTENTS

■ COVER. Luque, Kempes and Bertoni, and all of Argentina celebrate ■ TITLE PAGE. The famous paper storm is the background to this pyramidal struggle ■ TOP. 'We did it,' he tells the world ■ MIDDLE. They did it: Passarella and Fillol foil Neeskens ■ BOTTOM. They did it all for this.

INTRODUCTION
BY RON GREENWOOD

I left Argentina with mixed feelings. On the one hand, I found the 1978 World Cup finals an invigorating experience and a signpost to better days in the game. On the other, I was saddened because I was only an observer and not directly involved. Saddened, too, because there were players back in England who could have made their marks in Argentina and got some idea of what football at this level is all about. I am not prepared to guess at what England might have done in these finals because I don't like hypothetical questions. All one can do is evaluate and compare, asking oneself: 'Can we do this or do that?' You have got to be open-minded. It is wrong to say we have nothing to learn from others. That is why England were on the outside looking in this time. I like to feel we are all capable of learning. Any side fortunate enough to have qualified certainly ought to benefit from the experience.

The tournament struck me as being most interesting and entertaining. Though there was a distinct shortage of star personalities, the level of skilful, combined work was high and the two principal attacking sides got to the final. That has got to be good for the game and for its future. There has been criticism of the league system used in the second round, but I think the format is all right as it is. It certainly encouraged attacking football this time. Overall, too, I felt the refereeing was good and that the competition was played in the most sporting manner in a country where trouble was expected on the field. No-one can speak too highly of the Argentinian public, either. Sporting and well-behaved, they celebrated in a way that was as free of trouble as it was high-spirited.

Tactically, the finals suggested that defensive trends have gone forever. I should certainly like to think so, anyway. The cycle does appear to be on the up-swing, and I should hope the good things about this World Cup will spill over into the league football of every country in the world. We have all got to be more adventurous. I'd like to see coaches encouraging players to become more creative. A lot of bad coaching has restricted and retarded talent. Football is both a simple and a complex game. Coaches won't let people make the odd mistake; but players must be encouraged to take on opponents. In fact, one of the weaknesses of this World Cup was the lack of individualistic players.

As far as we in England are concerned, we have obviously got to concentrate more on working with the ball. Good technique at high speed was the keynote in Argentina, and we have got to practise doing things the hard way, if you like. We must learn to cope instantly with the bad pass as well as the good one; and that means looking closely at our technique and skill. Our centre backs could deal all day with high balls, but they would be flummoxed by some of the quick one-twos we saw in Argentina. The one-two is not new by any means, but it has gone out of our game. I last saw it used in England by Arthur Rowe's push-and-run side at Spurs. Football is all about time and space. We have become past masters at shutting up space, but we have forgotten how to create it and how to use it.

We have got to encourage players to perfect their techniques, to develop a touch and to get a feel for the ball. You are never going to replace players like Johan Cruyff and Franz Beckenbauer exactly because they were absolutely unique. But someone is going to come along and take their places. Holland got to the World Cup final without Cruyff, and

Introduction by Ron Greenwood

it is one of those 'The king is dead. Long live the king!' situations in world football now. There is always someone around the corner, as Mario Kempes proved, and I should like to feel we have one or two budding stars ourselves in England. Hopefully, they will make the world sit up and take notice in Spain in 1982.

It would certainly be nice to be directly involved. Unless you are, you cannot fully appreciate the World Cup atmosphere and all the stresses and strains that go with it. At managerial level it means you have got to have a lot of dignity and stature – particularly dignity. The eyes of the world are upon you. So, put one foot wrong and the whole world knows about it. Qualification also places certain burdens and responsibilities on players' shoulders. They must be prepared to accept they are about to become involved in an unusual situation – that of being encamped together over a long period. If they don't arrive with the right attitude there is bound to be trouble. Equally, of course, they must be prepared pyschologically for the experience by their manager.

WORLD CUP ARGENTINA?

Argentina '78 was not, in all honesty, the most promising of World Cup finals. Explosive politically and denied the greatest playing talents of the day, it threatened us with more trouble and less entertainment than any of its ten predecessors. In short, it looked to have all the capacity to delight of a double hernia.

Psychologically, its major handicap was the unpredictable and, to many, distasteful political situation in the host country. Though the urban terrorists of the Left had been stamped on ruthlessly during the two years of military rule by Lieutenant-General Jorge Rafael Videla's junta, the threat of violence remained very real when the 16 finalists began to assemble, a little uneasily in some cases, in Argentina at the end of May.

Only a few weeks before the start of the tournament, one policeman had been killed and another injured as they tried to remove a bomb planted in the Buenos Aires Press Centre. It was a disturbing incident not only in simple human terms but also in view of the pledge given a year earlier by the Montoneros, one of the two principal terrorist groups, that they would not interfere with the 'Mundial', the Argentinian abbreviation for the 1978 World Cup finals, because it was a 'festival of the people'.

That reassuring public announcement was welcome if only because, ever since the previous World Cup finals in West Germany four years earlier, Europe had harboured serious misgivings about the choice by FIFA, the governing body of world football, of Argentina as the venue for 1978. It certainly went some way towards allaying the fears aroused by the assassination in 1976 of General Actis, the newly-appointed president of Ente Autarquico Mundial (EAM), a few hours before his inaugural Press conference as head of Argentina's World Cup organization. But when

> **What Liberalism mounted was a campaign of its own—counter-productive to a large extent—to balance the junta's obvious intention of using the finals as a massive public relations exercise.**

that bomb went off in Buenos Aires, it began to look as though the terrorists had decided that, after all, the finals presented them with an opportunity of stating their case to the world that was simply too good to miss.

Liberals the world over had come to that conclusion long before West Germany, the reigning world champions, and Poland got these finals under way with the inaugural match in Buenos Aires on June 1. Amnesty International, the organization dedicated to the preservation of human rights, were the most active. Journalists bound for Argentina were bombarded beforehand with Amnesty literature, carefully documented, reminding them of the alleged atrocities, including torture and imprisonment without trial, carried out by the junta in their campaign to wipe out terrorism and restore order to a South American nation that was on the brink of civil war before the military coup in 1976. Britain's National Union of Journalists, too, urged its members reporting the World Cup not to gloss over the more unpleasant facts of life in Argentina.

Sensibly, there was no attempt to persuade sports writers not to cover the

event (indeed, many of them were deeply offended by the implication that they had no knowledge of world affairs). What Liberalism mounted was a campaign of its own – counter-productive to a large extent – to balance the junta's obvious intention of using the finals as a massive public relations exercise. Extremely sensitive to European opinion – it is said that an Argentinian is someone born in Italy who speaks Spanish and thinks he is an Englishmen – Argentina's military leaders had complained constantly and bitterly about the 'distortion' of their country's image on the other side of the Atlantic. So this classic case of mixing politics with sport represented, quintessentially, Argentina's longing for credibility in the eyes of the world, and in those of Europe most particularly. To gain it, the junta were prepared to pay the earth. An American public relations firm, Burson-Marsteller, was hired to polish Argentina's image at a fee of $1 million a year, and early estimates of the total cost of staging the finals ranged from a staggering £340 million to a stupendous £700 million. The higher figure was twice as much as it cost West Germany, a much more affluent nation, to stage the 1972 Olympic Games, and even the lower figure outstripped the West Germans' outlay on the 1974 World Cup finals by a

■ PREVIOUS, ABOVE AND OVER. The junta's apprehension, their relief and delight are shown against the background of the opening ceremony ■ INSET. Rebuilding the River Plate Stadium and its use in the final.

cool £300 million or so. To be fair, such comparisons do not take into account the fact that, to play hosts to the world, Argentina had to build and rebuild stadia and install telecommunications facilities to a far greater degree than the sophisticated West Germans.

For the first time in the history of the World Cup, the host country had to build three completely new stadia: those at Mendoza, Cordoba and Mar del Plata, and substantially remodel another three, the River Plate and Velez Sarsfield in Buenos Aires and that at Rosario. Because the hosts were required to provide television coverage of the finals in colour, it was necessary, too, for Argentina to revamp its somewhat primitive black and white domestic system. So, within six months of taking power, the junta had created a state colour television production company, Argentina '78 TV, and had laid the foundation stone of a sprawling and costly television centre near the heart of Buenos Aires. From there, the matches were beamed by satellite to the rest of the world in colour while the Argentinians themselves continued to watch in black and white. In addition, improvements on a similar scale had to be made to Argentina's Heath Robinson telephone and telex networks so that newspaper reporters could cover the finals adequately.

So much work was necessary, in fact, that a full-scale government row broke out at one point over the escalating costs of trying to do in two years what should have been done in four. It was sparked off by the Treasury Secretary, Juan Alemann, who spoke out against the colossal expense with a bravery few would care to show in a country where at least 5000 dissidents were said to have disappeared without trace since the coup of 1976. Worried about Argentina's alarming rate of inflation, once 900 per cent annually and still running as high as 165 per cent per annum at the time of the World Cup, Alemann called the cost of staging the finals 'the most visible and indefensible case of non-priority spending in Argentina today'.

What the Treasury Secretary failed totally to recognize, of course, was that the 1978 World Cup finals had virtually become the junta's *raison d'être*. But for the military, certainly, and their impressive acceleration of the World Cup preparations that had stagnated under the preceding Peronist regime, FIFA might well have been swayed by the European criticism of Argentina's state of preparedness and switched the venue to Mexico, Brazil or Spain, the alternatives mooted at the time. Without doubt, Argentina kept these finals only because the junta set up EAM to run the show with a degree of efficiency and precision for which Argentinian administration had not been exactly famous previously.

In a sense, Argentina's military government staked all on the tournament. It was hardly a straightforward case of win or bust, but their reputation did come to depend very heavily on presenting to the world finals that were not only smoothly run and trouble-free but also vividly memorable. And there, in that latter respect, they were completely at the mercy of the 16 teams who had either earned or been accorded the right to challenge for the title of world champions. While the junta could concentrate Argentina's resources on making the finals work and flood the World Cup centres with troops and police to deter the terrorists, the one thing that was beyond their power was to order the teams to play well.

World Cup Argentina?

Unfortunately for them, too, Argentina '78 coincided with a sudden dearth of conspicuously gifted, world class players. Indeed, these finals began as the show without a star. There should have been two, West Germany's Franz Beckenbauer and Holland's Johan Cruyff; but Beckenbauer, *Der Kaiser*, had abdicated to join American soccer's gold rush, while Cruyff, another target for the Yankee speculators in his early retirement, seemed simply to have had enough of the pressures in the goldfish bowl of international football. Whatever the reasons, Beckenbauer and Cruyff did not go with their national teams to Argentina, and the finals seemed certain to be immeasurably poorer for the absence of the world's two leading players.

Nor were they the only distinguished absentees. West Germany had to defend their title without Paul Breitner, Wolfgang Overath, Uli Höness, Gerd Müller and Jurgen Grabowski as well as the peerless Beckenbauer; injury added Giacinto Facchetti to the long list of famous 1974 names missing from the 1978 Italian squad; and Wim van Hanegem, Cruyff's lieutenant when Holland lost unexpectedly to West Germany in the final of the 1974 World Cup, pulled out this time when he discovered he could not be guaranteed a regular place in the side.

Those who were left did not appear to add up to much. Brazil still had Roberto Rivelino's marvellous left foot; Kazimierz Deyna continued to orchestrate Poland subtly from midfield; and there was a chance that West Germany's Rainer Bonhof would recapture the form which burst upon the 1974 finals like a shell. Even so, genuine talent looked to be so thinly spread that it practically required psychic powers to name the eventual winners, or even the two finalists, in advance. No team stood out, and the title of world champions was there for the taking. Rarely, it seemed, had there been a more open World Cup. But the levelling-down process that many insisted had taken place since the thrilling European Championship two years earlier brought with it a moment of opportunity for teams and individuals alike. Where better to prove star quality that on the biggest World Cup stage of all? The material was there, we suspected, in promising aspirants like Holland's Rob Rensenbrink, Brazil's Zico, Italy's Roberto Bettega and Franco Causio, France's Michel Platini, Argentina's Leopoldo Luque, Austria's Hans Krankl and Scotland's Kenny Dalglish. All had suggested before the finals that they had what it took to become a household name around the world.

At the same time, however, there was a deep-rooted fear in Europe that any violence in Argentina would not be confined to activities off the field. As we had seen in numerous brutal matches for the World Club Championship, Argentinian and European football had never mixed well. They represented two totally different philosophies about the game, and the cynicism of the one and the robustness of the other were a potentially explosive combination. Nor was there any great confidence that all the World Cup referees, exposed to the extreme passion and partisanship of volatile Argentine crowds, would have the strength of character to give the more skilful players the protection from destructive tackling they needed to express their gifts.

Thus, fearful of bloodshed on and off the field, hoping against hope that the World Cup would again use its magical powers to give us at least one new player to drool over and insulated against the chill of an Argentinian autumn by the warmth of the Argentinian people, we waited expectantly for Argentina '78 to prove that pessimism unfounded on all counts.

W. GERMANY V POLAND

As a pipe-opener to the tournament, this promising pairing of the reigning world champions and the team which finished third in 1974 was an unmitigated disaster. For the fourth World Cup in succession, the inaugural match failed to produce a single goal and the two sides succeeded only in boring a tolerant capacity crowd of 78,000 half to death. The joke of the week in Buenos Aires was that the tedious, long-winded and ultimately sterile FIFA Congress at the Sheraton Hotel had provided better entertainment and, if any more evidence were required to prove that the finals should again begin *en bloc,* this match was it.

The trouble with inaugural matches is that they have to follow a lavish opening ceremony – indeed they are an excuse for it – and must take place in atmosphere overloaded with tension and pressure of all kinds, not the least being that of nationalism. Starting a World Cup is a nervous enough moment in itself, but to be expected to set a high tone for the rest of the tournament as well as asking too much of the unfortunate teams involved. West Germany and Poland, certainly, found the burden too great to bear.

Having proved during the first half that their defence, built around the immovable Gorgon and Zmuda, was sturdy enough to cope with anything the West Germans could offer, Poland attacked strongly for most of the second half. Still blessed with some electric acceleration, Lato ran his marker, Zimmerman, to distraction and the midfield subtleties of Deyna, clearly the man of the match, were often beyond West Germany's comprehension.

Halfway through the second half, Deyna nearly scored one goal and made another. Maier did well to save from the Polish captain with his feet after

Lubanski had pulled the ball back from the byline and then, two minutes later, Szarmach failed by inches to touch in at the far post another of Deyna's cunning free kicks. Indeed, if Lubanski and Szarmach had played to form, there is little doubt that Poland would have won. As it was, they tired noticeably late in the game and Boniek and Kasperczak were sent on to replace Lubanski and Masztaler respectively.

The final whistle arrived with the crowd whistling and booing in their frustration at not having seen a goal. Most of their dissatisfaction, without doubt, was directed at West Germany, who had played with a sloppiness totally foreign to them. Flohe, in particular, could not put a pass right all afternoon on a pitch, scheduled to take the World Cup final, that was ominously bumpy after being watered with sea water by mistake and hurriedly relaid.

It was not unusual for West Germany to begin a World Cup unimpressively.

They were beaten by East Germany in the first round, for instance, before going on to win the 1974 World Cup, and their veteran manager, Helmut Schön, talked this time of wanting a slow build-up with the minimum of effort. Some, however, took West Germany's inept performance as additional proof of their decline, just as others were convinced that West Germany and Poland had deliberately contrived a draw in order to make absolutely sure of a place for themselves in the last eight.

West Germany: Maier, Vogts, Rüssmann, Kaltz, Zimmerman, Bonhof, Beer, Flohe, H. Müller, Abramczik, Fischer.

Poland: Tomaszewski, Maculewicz, Gorgon, Zmuda, Szymanowski, Nawalka, Deyna, Masztaler (Kasperczak 84 min.), Lato, Lubanski (Boniek 79 min.), Szarmach.

Referee: Angel Coerezza (Argentina).

■ OPPOSITE. Lato watches Zimmerman and Rüssmann outjump his team-mate ■ Lato shadows Flohe ■ ABOVE. Szarmach and Zimmermann portray the feelings of those who had to watch this match.

GROUP ONE

The devil himself could not have devised a more fiendish World Cup group than this. The throwing together of four of the stronger teams, like cats in a bag, was only the work of FIFA, however, with the help of a little political manoeuvring by West Germany and Italy. It seemed crazy to threaten the host nation, the biggest money-spinner, so dangerously at such an early stage.

A lot of muddled thinking was involved. For a start, FIFA decided in their wisdom that Holland's appearance in the final of the 1974 World Cup carried more weight than Italy's record of having won the World Cup twice, albeit before the war, and having reached the final in 1970. So Holland, and not Italy, were accorded the fourth seeded place in company with Argentina, West Germany and Brazil. The problem then was where to put Italy. West Germany did not want them in Group Two and the Italians finally opted for Group One on the assumption that the host nation would be given a relatively easy passage into the second round. FIFA themselves described the placing of Italy as compensation for missing the fourth seeded spot. Some compensation, as it turned out, some draw.

As for the quality of the four teams, it was difficult to judge Argentina's true worth because, as hosts, they qualified automatically. Nor did patchy results in a protracted series of warm-up matches give much of a clue to what could be expected of them in June 1978. The previous summer, for

> "But the host nation always does we traditionally. Everything is in the favour. Even the referees are und the influence of the crowds..."

instance, they had tested themselves in Buenos Aires against seven touring European nations with the following results: Poland 3–1, West Germany 1–3, England 1–1, Scotland 1–1, France 0–0, Yugoslavia 1–0 and East Germany 2–0. More encouraging for them was an earlier 5–1 victory over Hungary, but allowances had to be made for the fact that Hungary had fielded a below-strength side at the end of a tiring South American tour.

The constant factor in Argentina's preparation was the brave attempt by their young manager, Cesar Luis Menotti, to alter radically the style and ethos of his country's football. At the start of this World Cup Menotti had been in charge for three years—a post-war record for management of Argentina—and, from the beginning, he insisted the tournament could be won by playing skilful, attacking football. Saying it and doing it were two entirely different things.

Above all, Menotti had overcome the cynical, defensive attitude that, encouraged by coaches like Juan Carlos Lorenzo, the man who had been in charge of the notorious Argentina World Cup side of 1966, had permeated the country's football at every level and which, arguably, had cost them the major prize in England. Menotti had to do it, too, without many of Argentina's most gifted players.

The country's galloping inflation had caused a mass exodus of them to the more financially rewarding leagues of Europe, and the Argentina FA was slow to respond to Menotti's plea for a ban on transfers abroad. Nor was it easy to get the exiles back. In the end, the only one Menotti managed to retrieve was Mario Kempes, and it cost $25,000 to secure the prolific striker's release from his Spanish club, Valencia.

If Menotti was entitled to curse his luck, so was, to a lesser extent, Enzo Bearzot, the manager of Italy. Injury robbed him of Giacinto Facchetti, his extremely experienced captain and sweeper between the end of the qualifying competition with England, Finland and Luxembourg and the start of the finals, and a loss of form during the same period suggested that Italy might have given of their best already in edging England out of Argentina '78 on goal difference. A month before the finals, and facing mounting criticism from the Italian Press, Bearzot admitted pessimistically that this World Cup might have come one year too late or one year too early for a team he suddenly found he had to reshape quickly.

The job was done brilliantly. Gaetano Scirea was chosen to succeed Facchetti and soon struck up an understanding with Mauro Bellugi at the centre of the defence. Marco Tardelli, quick, mobile and combative, was moved from full back to midfield while Antonio Cabrini, a virtually unknown youngster, was brought in successfully to take over from Tardelli. Finally, Bearzot satisfied his critics by preferring Paolo Rossi, the expensive goal-scoring prodigy of Italian football, to Francesco Graziani in attack. Despite the changes, however, Italy began the finals with a team containing no fewer than eight Juventus players, Bellugi, Antognoni and Rossi being the odd men out.

Bearzot set out to lessen the national team's dependence on *catenaccio* (blanket) defence and the counter-attack. In place of those traditional, and often sterile tactics, he promoted the concept of flexibility and versatility. In other words, Bearzot wanted Italy to attack when they could and defend only when they had to.

Michel Hidalgo, the manager of France, did not have half as much to prove as either Menotti or Bearzot. Nevertheless, Argentina '78 was important to French football as a measure of the recovery of the country's game. Sponsorship and an influx of overseas players had brought it back to life, and fond memories of Kopa and Fontaine in 1958 made the world keen to see what France could do on their first appearance in the World Cup finals since 1966.

A determined 1–0 victory over Brazil in Paris by a severely depleted French team had suggested they were capable of making their presence felt in Argentina, particularly when they could call on high class players like Platini, Bathenay and Tresor all at the same time. St Etienne's progress in European club football and success in a qualifying group with Bulgaria and the Republic of Ireland had shown that French football was on the move: now Argentina waited to see how far it could go.

Like France, Hungary were on the way back after last appearing in the World Cup finals in 1966, and their route to Argentina had proved they certainly did not lack courage or resilience. Having overcome Russia, their bogey side, and Greece in a European qualifying group, Hungary then had to take part in a playoff with Bolivia to reach Group One. There could be no question, either, about the quality of their leadership. The man in charge, Lajos Baroti, had been part of football for 46 years and was participating in the World Cup for the fourth time. He was, in fact, a direct link with and a living reminder of, the palmy days of Hungarian football in the 1950s.

Asked to name the likely winners of the 1978 World Cup before Hungary's 4–1 defeat by England at Wembley the week before the World Cup, Baroti singled out Holland and West Germany before adding: 'But the host nation always does well traditionally. Everything is in their favour. Even the referees are under the influence of the home crowds. . . .'

Cesar Luis Menotti

FRANCE V ITALY

There could have been no more spectacular or encouraging opening to Group One than the goal Bernard Lacombe scored for France after less than a minute of the first match at the seaside resort of Mar Del Plata, 250 miles to the south of Buenos Aires. A swift interchange of passes in the French half suddenly produced a glorious long ball down the left and sent Six racing away down to the byeline. The winger's cross was measured to perfection and Lacombe, no giant, timed his jump better than the taller Italian defenders to steer the ball wide of Zoff with a classic centre forward's scoring header.

It was a rapier thrust which, understandably, encouraged France to believe that, even without the unfit Bathenay and Rocheteau, they had the beating of Italy. It certainly looked that way for a while as the Italian defence kept being caught out by high crosses and Lacombe, a little man with a big jump, headed a free-kick narrowly wide. If, we thought, the Italians' suspect temperament is going to let them down in the World Cup, now is the moment it is going to happen.

The winger's cross was measured to perfection and Lacombe, no giant, timed his jump better than the taller Italian defenders to steer the ball wide of Zoff with a classic centre forward's scoring header.

It did not principally because of one man, Romeo Benetti. In that perilous moment of crisis for Italy, the craggy, 32-year old Juventus midfield player rallied his team brilliantly by winning control of the midfield for them and sending the forwards on the attack. It was Benetti's centre that enabled Bettega to force Bertrand-Demanes into a diving save after 25 minutes, and it was the confidence that Benetti had generated that produced Italy's somewhat bizarre equalizing goal five minutes later.

When the ball was crossed from the left, Bettega sliced his attempted volley but Causio, coming in from the right, managed to head against the bar. The rebound clipped Causio as the momentum of his run carried him into the goal-mouth, and the ball eventually went into the net off Rossi, who was just behind Causio. From then until the last five minutes it was all Italy.

Bertrand-Demanes had to save from Benetti and Bettega before the interval, and, six minutes the other side of the break, Italy took what proved to be a decisive lead. Zaccarelli, who had replaced Antognoni in midfield at the restart, celebrated by driving a low, first time shot past Bertrand-Demanes when Rossi pulled the ball back to him invitingly. Italy's Tardelli and France's Platini were booked as the French fought to get back into the game, but Italy's superiority was threatened only by dangerous shots from Bossis and Guillou in the closing minutes.

France: Bertrand-Demanes, Janvion, Rio, Tresor, Bossis, Michel, Guillou, Platini, Dalger, Lacombe (1) (Berdoll 72 min.), Six (Rouyer 76 min.).

Italy: Zoff, Gentile, Bellugi, Scirea, Cabrini, Tardelli, Benetti, Antognoni (Zaccarelli 46 min. (1)), Causio, Rossi (1), Bettega.

Referee: Nicolas Rainea (Romania).

■ Tresor and Betrand-Demanes watch Michel advance towards Antognoni and Tardelli with Platini in support ■ Tardelli lunges at Platini ... but Platini races clear to face Benetti. Rossi, Rio and Tresor look on as Michel runs wide and Tardelli is left behind.

HUNGARY V ARGENTINA

JUNE 2 BUENOS AIRES GROUP 1   HUNGARY 1 ARGENTINA 2

Here, we were brought face to face with the full force of Argentina's raging desire to win the World Cup for the first time and on their own soil. The scene when the teams emerged was overwhelming. The crowd of 75,000 went off like a bomb, their chants of 'Ar-gen-tina, Ar-gen-tina' battering the senses into submission and the ticker-tape coming down from the packed top tier of this majestic stadium like a blizzard. The frenzy and the delight were mirrored, too, in the pace of a superb contest that, coming the day after the severely disappointing inaugural match on the same pitch, threw into harsh relief the failure of West Germany and Poland to entertain.

Sadly, in view of the sense of occasion and the extremely high technical quality

of the play, the game was to end in violence and recrimination. Poorly refereed by the Portuguese, Antonio Garrido, it was marred by several bad fouls, for two of which Hungary's Torocsik and Nyilasi were rightly sent off during the last three minutes. 'We are just as hard as anybody else,' Baroti had warned before Wembley, and in this game Hungary proved it disturbingly. They began the ill-feeling by chopping opponents down early in the game, and Baroti could apologize afterwards for Torocsik and Nyilasi only by asking for their youth and the tension of the occasion to be taken into account.

What Baroti did not mention was the frustration and feeling of injustice that clearly engulfed the Hungarian players towards the end. For the result had been in doubt until seven minutes from time, when Bertoni, one of the two substitutes brought on by Argentina, steered the ball into an empty net after it

had broken loose from a head-on collision between Gujdar and Kereki of Hungary and Luque as the Argentina striker chased a through pass into the heart of the Hungarian defence. But only 13 minutes earlier, however, Nagy had nearly scored the winner for Hungary. Under pressure, Csapo laid off a delicate pass to Martos, substituting for the injured Torok at right back, and Nagy did everything perfectly with his head except guide Martos' centre the right side of a post. There is little doubt, therefore, that the two contrasting incidents were uppermost in the Hungarian mind when Torocsik, who had received some rough treatment from the Argentinian defence as well, took a kick at Gallego and then Nyilasi went over the top in tackling Tarantini.

■ OPPOSITE. Gujdar and Kereki foil Luque, but not Bertoni . . .
■ ABOVE. Hungarians huddle in celebration after Csapo's goal ■ Torocsik's long lonely walk.

Hungary V Argentina

The referee had no alternative. Not only did the fouls themselves merit dismissal, both Hungarians had been booked earlier, Nyilasi for a foul on Valencia and Torocsik for dissent. Even so, Garrido cannot escape all of the blame for what happened. He let far too many fouls go unpunished, and he never appeared to be fully in control of a game that was, admittedly, difficult to referee because of its tremendous pace.

Perhaps the most encouraging feature of it all was the unusual restraint shown by Argentina in the face of severe provocation. It was not until quite late in the game that they, once notorious for the viciousness of their play, began to retaliate at all seriously. Throughout the 90 minutes they were guilty of only two truly unpalatable offences, one of them a waist-high tackle by Passarella on Pinter that threatened to cut the Hungarian midfield player in half.

In the main, Argentina simply concentrated on showing that they could play their short-passing game at great speed and with devastating accuracy. In no time at all, too, it became clear that, in Kempes and Luque, Argentina had discovered an attacking partnership that could win the World Cup for them. Almost indistinguishable from each other with their long black hair, searing pace and ability to control the ball deftly at speed, this tall pair immediately struck up an understanding that was astonishing in view of Kempes' late arrival on the World Cup scene. Significantly, Luque equalized for Argentina after 14 minutes by applying the finishing touch to a thunderous Kempes shot that Gujdar could not hold.

As for Hungary, they were completely unrecognizable as the side which had defended badly, attacked only sporadically and played with little or no enthusiasm against England at Wembley. Here they attacked Argentina as hard and as skilfully as Argentina attacked them, and only 10 minutes had gone when they strung together a lovely four-man move. Fillol could only parry Zombori's fierce shot and Csapo ran the rebound into the net to give Hungary a start completely at odds with their finish.

Argentina: Fillol, Olguin, L. Galvan, Passarella, Tarantini, Ardiles, Gallego, Valencia (Alonso 75 min.), Houseman (Bertoni 67 min.(1)), Kempes, Luque (1).
Hungary: Gujdar, Torok (Martos 46 min.), Kereki, Kocsis, J. Toth, Pinter, Nyilasi, Zombori, Csapo (1), Torocsik, Nagy.
Referee: Antonio Garrido (Portugal).

■ OPPOSITE. Nagy fails to block Olguin's shot ■ Battle for the ball at River Plate ■ CLOCKWISE FROM TOP LEFT. Ardiles and Pinter, Alonso and Pinter, Tarantini and Meszaros, Kempes and Martos ■ ABOVE. Luque and Bertoni celebrate the winning goal as Gujdar lies injured after colliding with Luque and Kereki.

ITALY V HUNGARY

The difference in quality between Italy and Hungary beside the seaside was not measured accurately by the scoreline. In addition to their three goals, Italy could point to the three occasions on which Bettega hit the bar and numerous other near-misses as a truer picture of their all-round superiority. Weakened by the one match suspension automatically imposed on Torocsik and Nyilasi for their misdemeanours against Argentina, and still without their injured winger, Varadi, Hungary were ill-equipped to cope with the Italians in their new, determined, attacking mood.

Once again, Benetti was the man of the match. To the surprise of many, the player once known as 'the Assassin' because of his propensity for cutting down opponents, Benetti proved for the second game running that he was just as adept at using the ball intelligently as he was at winning it. It was fitting, therefore, that he should score Italy's third goal with a fine shot on the hour to complement those by Rossi (34 min.) and Bettega (35 min.) in the first half. Hungary's goal, a penalty by Andras Toth, was not scored until ten minutes from the end.

Italy: Zoff, Gentile, Bellugi, Scirea, Cabrini (Cuccureddu 79 min.), Tardelli, Benetti (1), Antognoni, Causio, Rossi (1), Bettega (1) (Graziani 83 min.).

Hungary: Meszaros, Martos, Kocsis, Kereki, J. Toth, Pinter, Fazekas (A. Toth 46 min. (pen.)), Zombori, Csapo, Pusztai, Nagy (Halasz 46 min.).

Referee: Ramon Baretto (Uruguay).

■ Benetti and Bettega celebrate: Italy qualify for the next round.

ARGENTINA V FRANCE

Bobby Charlton, veteran of many a stirring contest himself, went so far as to call this 'the finest international match I have ever seen', and few would argue with the celebrated former England player, who was in Argentina as an expert voice with BBC Television. The entertainment value was incalculable as Argentina and France attacked each other brilliantly at high speed. Argentina won the scrap in the end, but no team deserved elimination less than France. Indeed, this World Cup was all the poorer for the departure this second narrow defeat forced upon the French.

What made it all the worse was that France were manifestly unfortunate to lose to Argentina. For the referee, Jean Dubach of Switzerland, was more than a little generous awarding Argentina the first half penalty with which they took the lead and a lot more than mean when he refused France a similar award for a clear trip from behind on Six during the second half. All of a sudden, Lajos Baroti's warning about referees favouring the host nation under the influence of the home crowds came flooding back.

Not even dubious refereeing, however, could obscure the essential quality of the match. Strengthened by the return of Bathenay, Rocheteau and Battiston and the introduction of Lopez, France played with great authority and enterprise. Their one-touch football was a delight. Tresor, the coloured player from Marseilles, looked to be the most accomplished World Cup defender since Bobby Moore in Mexico eight years ago and France might easily have drawn if their goalkeeper, Bertrand-Demanes had not been carried off injured early in the second half, and Six had not missed a sitter halfway through it.

All that France lacked to beat Argentina was a Luque or a Kempes. For all his success in the air against Italy and his skill on the ground in this match, Lacombe was not the battering ram France needed to finish off their clever, progressive attacks. He and Rocheteau both missed good chances, for instance, before Luque ran up the curtain on his double act with Kempes with a shot that Lopez kicked off the line. Kempes then volleyed against Bertrand-Demanes' legs and nearly broke a post in two with a later shot of awesome power.

■ Tresor leads his defence against Ardiles and Kempes
■ OVER. Ardiles makes the opening for Luque's volley which leaves Baratelli helpless.

Argentina V France

Indeed, Argentina were well into the gallop when Kempes passed two men in midfield and sent Luque darting into the French penalty area. The ubiquitous Tresor challenged him and there were loud Argentinian protests that the defender had handled the ball at the same time. It looked to be a case of involuntary handball but the referee pointed to the penalty spot after consulting a linesman on the other side of the field. Passarella, he of the mighty shot, gave the kick all he had got, and Argentina went 1–0 up on the stroke of half time.

Disaster struck France again when, 11 minutes into the second half, Bertrand- Demanes damaged his back against a post as he came to earth after tipping over the bar a venomous, dipping volley by Valencia. But things took a distinct turn for the better in the 61st minute when Lacombe lobbed the ball against Argentina's bar and Platini thumped the rebound irresistibly past Fillol.

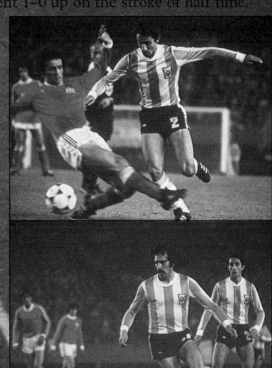

Platini then threatened to turn the match with a magnificent run and pass, but Six rolled the ball wide after running clear and drawing the goalkeeper. That was to be France's last chance and a costly miss. With 16 minutes left to play, the French defence stood off Luque, whom they obviously expected to bring the ball under control as he turned just outside their penalty area. Instead, Luque exploded into an audacious volley that surprised no-one more than Baratelli, France's substitute goalkeeper, who dived for the shot like a man in a dream.

The price Argentina had to pay for this victory was high. Alonso, brought on once more as a midfield substitute for Valencia, was hurt almost immediately and had to go off again. But the most serious blow of all was the dislocated elbow suffered by the irreplaceable Luque late in the game. Would he be fit to play against Italy, emerging as the most complete team in the tournament, and Argentina's next opponents? We should have to wait and see.

Argentina: Fillol, Olguin. L. Galvan, Passarella (pen.), Tarantini, Ardiles, Gallego, Valencia (Alonso 65 min., Ortiz 73 min.), Houseman, Kempes, Luque (1).

France: Bertrand-Demanes (Baratelli 59 min.), Battiston, Lopez, Tresor, Bossis, Michel, Platini (1), Bathenay, Rocheteau, Lacombe, Six.

Referee: Jean Dubach (Switzerland).

■ ABOVE. The French team race up field ■ Kempes meets a strong French challenge.

FRANCE V HUNGARY

France, whose skill had already etched itself deep on these World Cup finals, left Argentina with a victory and a laugh to remember them by. The humour was provided by the sight of the French team playing in the green and white striped shirts of Mar Del Plata's Kimberley club, instead of in their own, because of a misunderstanding over which team should change its colours so that television viewers would not have to try to differentiate between France's blue and Hungary's red on black and white sets.

To cut a long and farcical story short, both teams turned up at Mar del Plata with their change strip of white, and an alternative had to be found in a hurry for France, the side supposed to be playing in their normal colours. Even so, the Kimberley shirts were not delivered to the ground in time for the scheduled 1.45 pm kick off, and the game eventually got under way 40 minutes late — to the horror, no doubt, of those whose job it is to arrange television programme schedules.

Understandably, with nothing at stake, both teams made changes of one kind or another – among them the inclusion of that French goalkeeper with the unfortunate name, Dropsy – and France ran up a 2–0 lead through Lopez and Berdoll after 36 minutes. Zombori struck back for Hungary four minutes later, but Rocheteau restored France's lead before half-time.

France: Dropsy, Janvion, Lopez (1), Tresor, Bracci, Petit, Bathenay, Papi (Platini 46 min.), Rocheteau (1) (Six 75 min.), Berdoll (1), Rouyer.

Hungary: Gujdar, Martos, Balint, Kereki, J. Toth, Pinter, Nyilasi, Pusztai, Zombori (pen.), Torocsik, Nagy (Csapo 73 min.).

Referee: Armando Cesar Coelho (Brazil).

■ ABOVE. Out of the cup but still smiling, just, Platini is greeted by Hidalgo ■ Dropsy fails to stop Zombori's shot.

ITALY V ARGENTINA

With this mature, economical victory in Argentina's own backyard, Italy established themselves firmly as the European side most likely to win the 1978 World Cup. Having taken the initiative against France and Hungary and attacked, they reverted here to their classic, counter-punching style of play that confirmed their versatility impressively.

In a sense, the Italians had no other tactical choice. Argentina's whole World Cup strategy was based on all-out attack whipped up to a frenzy by their howling fellow countrymen, and, as Hungary and France had discovered to their cost, it was inadvisable to try to fight fire with fire at the River Plate. So

Italy opted sensibly for the blanket defence and quick counter-attack for which, in the pre-Enzo Bearzot days, they had become famous, notorious even, the world over.

The plan worked perfectly. Argentina came at Italy like a gale in the first half, but the Italians took the buffeting without wilting and then broke out in the second half to score an exquisite and decisive goal that gave them maximum points in Group One. Also, of course, it forced Argentina to leave the River Plate, and all its advantages for them, and go to Rosario and Group B in the second round while Italy prepared to lord it in Buenos Aires and Group A as winners of Group One. Their right to such pre-eminence was indisputable. In their three first round matches, the Italians had proved themselves the best-equipped of the 16 finalists, both individually and collectively. Their teamwork was a model of precision and understanding, and Benetti, Bettega, Causio and Rossi each looked capable of becoming the outstanding player of the tournament. All of them, certainly, contributed fully to the triumph over Argentina, unbeaten previously at the River Plate.

Bettega's goal, scored in the 67th minute, was an absolute gem. It began with a swift, double interchange of passes between Antognoni (his major contribution to the game) and Rossi just outside Argentina's penalty area. And, while they were weaving their hypnotic spell on the defence, Bettega moved stealthily into a scoring position on the edge of the area itself. Rossi's final pass to him was sheer perfection, but Bettega still had to have the speed and courage to avoid Olguin's desperate flying tackle and the great goal-scorer's instinctive awareness of angles to screw his shot past Fillol as the goalkeeper came off his line.

■ ABOVE. Abraham Klein introduces Dino Zoff and Daniel Passarella ■ Bettega outjumped and outnumbered ■ OPPOSITE FROM TOP. Fillol gives directions ■ Gallego covers Ardiles as Rossi challenges ■ Olguin cowers beneath Bettega's flying feet ■ Passarella heads clear.

Italy V Argentina

Nor was that the first time Bettega had troubled Fillol. After 26 minutes of the first half, Italy had stolen out of defence to force a corner on the right. Causio took it. Rossi, so quick and neat in everything he did, back-headed the flag kick across the face of Argentina's goal and Bettega, leaping in the air to volley as he ran in full pelt towards goal, made the ball bounce wickedly in front of Fillol with a shot driven downwards. Only the quickness of the goal-keeper's reflexes enabled him to push the ball up over the bar.

Nevertheless, many were justified in believing that, overall, Benetti and Causio were more influential Italian figures than Bettega on the day. Both did an enormous amount of work without catching the eye as obviously as Bettega. Causio's pace was certainly vital to the success of Italy's counter-attacking, and Benetti shored up Italy in every moment of crisis quietly and efficiently from midfield. Well, perhaps not so quietly every time. The rugged Italian was booked on the hour for going for a bouncing ball with his foot as the unfortunate Ardiles tried to head it, and not all of Benetti's vigorous challenges were within the laws of the game.

Indeed, particularly while they were under siege in the first half, Italy often resorted to the spoiling tactics which are second nature to them. Yet the game was never allowed to get out of hand by the Israeli referee, Abraham Klein. Firm, fair and brave, Klein exercised a degree of control beyond Garrido of Portugal, and Dubach of Switzerland, the officials in charge of Argentina's matches against Hungary and France, and he twice refused to be intimidated by the crowd into awarding Argentina a penalty. Thus, thanks mainly to referee Klein, this climatic confrontation in Group One never looked like becoming the explosion of Latin violence many had feared and the applause of the Argentinian crowd for the Italian national anthem and the throwing of flowers to the crowd by the Italian players before the start were not made to appear mere empty gestures.

Ironically, one of Italy's early fouls ultimately even worked in their favour, though the possibility seemed remote when Bellugi, one of their established central defenders had to withdraw from the game after only seven minutes because he had aggravated a pre-match injury in bringing down Kempes. Cuccureddu, one of the nine Juventus players on the field now, was introduced to play at right back and release Gentile, one of the best tight markers in the business, to devote all his attention to the explosive Kempes.

The double burden of Gentile's adhesive presence and the absence of the injured Luque, the other half of Argentina's nuclear warhead, proved too great for Kempes to bear. Only twice did he look like saving the day for his team. In the 28th minute, Kempes very nearly beat Zoff in the top corner with a

Mr Klein keeps a close watch on Rossi and Tarantini ■ Passarella leads an attack on Zoff's goal ■ OPPOSITE. Passarella stops Bettega; illegally ■ Ardiles watches Benetti kick Gallego. Later, when Ardiles was kicked Benetti was booked.

Italy V Argentina

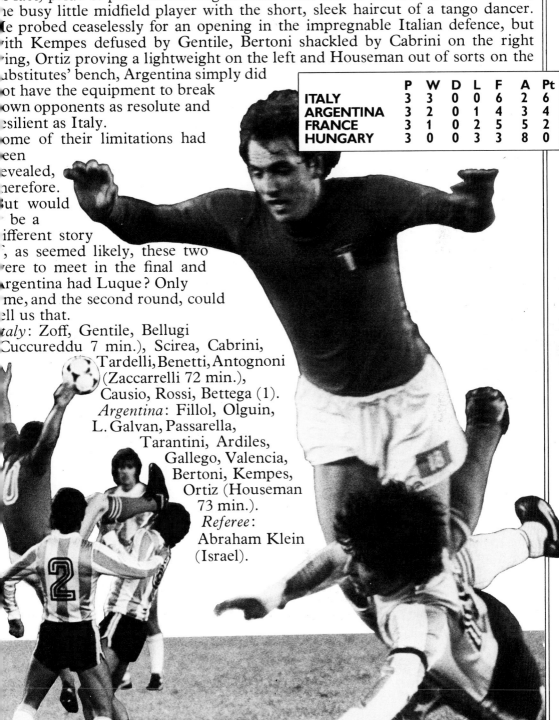

ipping, swerving free kick. (Zoff, incidently, also distinguished himself by
aving Passarella's powerful downward header from the ensuing corner kick.)
ive minutes later, Kempes volleyed Cuccureddu's misdirected header narrowly
'ide of a post.

n fact, pride of place in the Argentinian team had to be accorded to Ardiles,
ne busy little midfield player with the short, sleek haircut of a tango dancer.
Ie probed ceaselessly for an opening in the impregnable Italian defence, but
'ith Kempes defused by Gentile, Bertoni shackled by Cabrini on the right
'ing, Ortiz proving a lightweight on the left and Houseman out of sorts on the
ibstitutes' bench, Argentina simply did
ot have the equipment to break
own opponents as resolute and
esilient as Italy.

ome of their limitations had
een
evealed,
herefore.
ut would
be a
ifferent story
', as seemed likely, these two
'ere to meet in the final and
rgentina had Luque? Only
me, and the second round, could
ell us that.

taly: Zoff, Gentile, Bellugi
Cuccureddu 7 min.), Scirea, Cabrini,
Tardelli, Benetti, Antognoni
(Zaccarrelli 72 min.),
Causio, Rossi, Bettega (1).
Argentina: Fillol, Olguin,
L. Galvan, Passarella,
Tarantini, Ardiles,
Gallego, Valencia,
Bertoni, Kempes,
Ortiz (Houseman
73 min.).
Referee:
Abraham Klein
(Israel).

	P	W	D	L	F	A	Pt
ITALY	3	3	0	0	6	2	6
ARGENTINA	3	2	0	1	4	3	4
FRANCE	3	1	0	2	5	5	2
HUNGARY	3	0	0	3	3	8	0

GROUP TWO

W. GERMANY POLAND MEXICO TUNISIA

West Germany, the defending world champions, were certainly favoured by the first round draw. From the moment it was made, this group looked to be possibly the easiest and most uncomplicated of the four. So it proved – but not without one or two surprises along the way. To be frank, West Germany needed the most undemanding early matches they could get because their game had deteriorated steadily at both club and international level after the triumph over Holland in Munich four years earlier. That much was clear from the European club competitions and from West Germany's results and performances in the year immediately preceding the World Cup finals.

Essentially, the deterioration was a question of players, or rather the lack of them. Quite suddenly, the conveyor belt of exceptional talent which had supplied Helmut Schön, the West German manager, with Franz Beckenbauer, Uwe Seeler and Wolfgang Overath for the 1966 World Cup, Gerd Müller, Jurgen Grabowski and Bertie Vogts for Mexico in 1970 and Rainer Bonhof, Paul Breitner and Uli Höness for 1974 was offering mere mortals only instead of gods. The change did not become apparent, though, until quite late in the period between the 1974 and 1978 World Cups.

"There should be no place for such nations as Tunisia in the World Cup." But in the end, Tunisia were to have the last laugh.

To begin with, there seemed absolutely nothing to worry about. Gerd Müller retired from international football and Breitner went off to play in Spain, but Dieter Müller, one of the several promising youngsters West Germany were to unearth before Argentina '78 and Bernard Dietz looked to be perfectly adequate replacements at centre forward and left back. Indeed, the two of them were in the West German side beaten only on penalties by Czechoslovakia in the final of the memorable 1976 European Championship. The first alarm bell did not ring, in fact, until April, 1977, when it was reported that Beckenbauer was to leave Bayern Munich at the end of the Bundesliga season to join New York Cosmos and sign a three-year contract worth more than $1,500,000.

Even then, without Beckenbauer, West Germany emerged as the most successful of the many European sides which toured South America in the summer of 1977. Manny Kaltz, of Hamburg, though clearly lacking Beckenbauer's genius, looked to be a capable enough sweeper, Schalke's Klaus Fischer had shown on tour an appetite and instinct for goal-scoring similar to Gerd Müller's and Rudi Abramzcik was playing with sufficient pace and skill to suggest that the same club were about to supply the national team with a player in the great tradition of West German wingers. Nor was there any reason to reexamine that impression when Italy were beaten 2–1 in Berlin in October, 1977. The rot set in after that, West Germany's last impressive performance before Argentina '78.

First, the West Germans struggled to hold Wales to a 1–1 draw at Dortmund, then England went to West Germany in February, 1978, to play two friendlies, one a full international at Munich and the other a B international at Ausgburg. England at that point still very much on the road back under Ron Greenwood, led West Germany 1–0 for most of the senior match and lost 2–1 in the end only because of their own inexperience. In the B international, England won 2–1 against a West German team containing Erich Beer and Hansi Müller, two players destined for Argentina.

Even when allowances were made for the absence of Fischer, who could not play in the senior international because of influenza, and of the injured Dieter Müller and Höness, it was difficult not to conclude that West Germany no longer had the players to sustain their formidable reputation for skill, power and resilience. Unaccountably Bonhof had gone into his shell and now drove forward from midfield only in fits and starts. In 1974 he looked to have all the power, aggression, skill and personality to become West Germany's new leader, but his strange reluctance to take on the role from 1977 onwards made the loss of Beckenbauer's generalship all the more serious.

Worse was to follow. Brazil, bouncing back impressively from their 1–0 defeat by France in the opening match of their intensive European tour, beat West Germany 1–0 in Hamburg. Then, horror of horrors, the West Germans lost 3–1 away to Sweden, one of the unfancied qualifiers for Argentina. Schön kept insisting that results immediately before the World Cup finals meant little, that things were going according to plan and that, in effect, everything would be all right on the night. Many believed, however, that this time the kind, courteous man who had masterminded West German football for more than a decade was simply whistling in the dark.

Equally, few doubted that West Germany would qualify for the last eight in Argentina. They had, for instance, the psychological advantage over Poland and Mexico of never having lost to either of them.

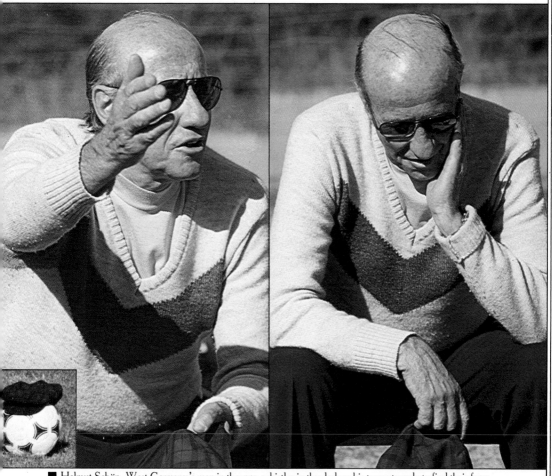

■ Helmut Schön, West Germany's man in the cap, whistles in the dark as his team struggle to find their form.

Group Two

Poland, however, were encouraged by the thought they had finished third in the 1974 World Cup and that their experience of the game at this rarified level was represented by nine survivors from the 1974 squad. Robert Gadocha was their only serious loss, but that promised to be made good by the return to international football of Wlodzimierz Lubanski, the dangerous striker whose career looked to have been ended by a crippling injury sustained against England during the 1974 qualifying competition.

Indeed, the attacking partnership of Lubanski, Lato and Szarmach was potentially the most effective in the 1978 World Cup. Lato, quick and deadly, finished the 1974 World Cup as its leading scorer with seven goals and Szarmach, then only 23, looked to have all the equipment necessary to achieve great things as a striker. With the graceful, intelligent Deyna still there behind them in midfield to supply the ammunition, there was every prospect of a lot of goals from Poland, scorers of 17 against Portugal, Denmark and Cyprus in their qualifying group – despite the toll four years had taken of some of them.

Mexico had toured Europe without distinction in preparation for Argentina, yet many good judges, among them Beckenbauer and his former international teammate, Gunter Netzer, believed the Mexicans were capable of upsetting the applecart in Group Two. They certainly had plenty of World Cup experience having failed to reach the finals only in 1934 and 1974, and there were justifiable hopes that the bearded, bushy-haired Leonardo Cuellar in midfield, Victor Rangel, a prolific striker, and Arturo Vasquez-Ayala their captain and reliable left|back would enable them to make their presence felt in Argentina. Doubts remained about the strength of their defence, though, and the quality of their opponents – the US, Canada, Haiti, El Salvador, Guatemala and Surinam – on their qualifying route to the finals did not inspire overwhelming confidence in Mexico.

There was none at all in Tunisia, one of those Third World countries which come to the World Cup finals as a completely unknown entity. A draw at home against Nigeria and a defeat in Egypt while qualifying tended to support the argument that there should be no place for such nations in the World Cup finals, particularly as the zonal qualifying system eliminated European sides of proven class such as England Czechoslovakia and Yugoslavia. The counter-argument, of course, is that the Third World must be allowed representation in order to encourage and develop the game outside Europe and South America. And, in the end, Tunisia were to have the last laugh

■ Szarmach, of Poland, scored 7 times in 1974, but failed to score in the opening match against West Germany.

TUNISIA V MEXICO

JUNE 2 ROSARIO GROUP 2 TUNISIA 3 MEXICO 1

Unrated Tunisia provided the 1978 World Cup with its first shock result on the first full day of the tournament. Totally underestimated by Mexico, the North African side came back after conceding a penalty, and being a goal down at half time, to score three times in the second half against vastly more experienced opponents. As *La Nacion,* one of the Buenos Aires newspapers, put it: 'Without doubt, this will go down in history as one of the most unexpected results of the 1978 World Cup. Few would have predicted it, but Tunisia have done it, and their victory puts them, for the moment, at the top of Group Two.'

Yes, it was a strange sight that – Tunisia sitting proudly above West Germany and Poland as well as an embarrassed Mexico. They deserved their moment of glory, though, because they proved themselves to be a faster, more purposeful and better integrated team than Mexico on the day. Cuellar and Hugo Sanchez rallied Mexico for a time, but their work was more than matched by Dhiab Tarak, outstanding for Tunisia in midfield, and by Naili, reassuringly secure in the Tunisian goal.

Essentially, however, it was an impressive team performance by Tunisia. Nothing could have revealed their character more thoroughly than the timing of Vasquez-Ayala's penalty for Mexico a minute before the end of a first half Tunisia had dominated. That no faults were found was demonstrated clearly by the second half goals from Ali Kaabi, Gommidh and Dhouib, men whose names suddenly became less unmanageable to European and South American tongues after a victory to compare with that of North Korea over Italy in 1966.

Tunisia: Naili, Dhouib (1), Gommidh (1), Jebali, Kaabi (1), Ben Rehaiem, M. Labidi, Dhiab, Lahzami Temime (K. Labidi 88 min.), Akid, R. Ben Aziza Karout 70 min.).

Mexico: Pilar-Reyes, Martinez, Tena, Ramos, Vasquez-Ayala (pen.), de la Torre, Cuellar, Mendizabal (Lugo 67 min.), Isiordia, Rangel, Sanchez.

Referee: John Gordon (Scotland).

■ Torre's pass evades Jebali as the two Labides look on.

POLAND V TUNISIA

Any assumptions that Tunisia's victory over Mexico had been just one of those freak results which occur from time to time in international football were dispelled completely by the trouble Poland had in winning at this industrial centre 250 miles up the River Plate from Buenos Aires.

Here, in this game, Tunisia proved conclusively that they were a cut above the average Third World side which reaches the World Cup finals. The Poles controlled the early stages of the game, but Tunisia dominated the last 20 minutes and deserved to draw a match which swung one way and then the other. Though a mistake by Mohsen Labidi allowed Lato to score Poland's winning goal three minutes before the interval, Tunisia's success in making their opponents sweat was based on a sound defensive performance that again drew attention to the skill of Naili in goal. When Tunisia did attack, however, they did so with such skill and force that mistakes were frequent in the experienced and redoubtable Polish defence. Dhiab, Tunisia's playmaker, hit the crossbar in the second half, and Jacek Gmoch, the Polish manager, had to urge his rattled players to calm down. It was a disappointing display by Poland, which looked slow alongside the tearaway Tunisians and which relied too heavily on the balding Lato for goals.

Each side had made one change for their second match in the group. While Poland retained Kasperczak, who had come on as substitute during the inaugural game against West Germany, in place of Masztaler, Tunisia brought in Gasmi for Raouf Ben Aziza. More significant, perhaps, were the two substitutions Poland made as Tunisia began to take control in the second half. Iwan, an out-and-out striker, and Boniek, a midfield striker, were sent on to replace the disappointing Szarmach and Lubanski in an attempt to give Lato more support up front.

Poland: Tomaszewski, Szymanowski, Gorgon, Zmuda, Maculewicz, Kasperczak, Deyna, Nawalka, Lato (1), Lubanski (Boniek 75 min.), Szarmach (Iwan 59 min.).
Tunisia: Naili, Dhouib, Gommidh, Jebali, Kaabi, Ben Rehaiem, M. Labidi, Dhiab, Lahzami Temime, Akid, Gasmi.
Referee: Angel Martinez (Spain).

■ Dhiab, Tunisia's midfield general, is closely watched by Szmanowski, Masztaier and Nawalka.

W.GERMANY V MEXICO

JUNE 6 CORDOBA GROUP 2   W. GERMANY 6 MEXICO 0

Suddenly, West Germany started scoring. Playing 450 miles north-west of Buenos Aires at Cordoba, a big, dusty industrial city surrounded by cattle ranches and with a view of the distant Andes, seemed to agree with them. Having made three changes in the team that laboured to that goalless draw with Poland the West Germans put four goals past Mexico in the first half and another two after the interval. And yet they still failed to impress with the overall quality of their play.

Most of the goals, scored by Flohe (two), Rummenigge (two), Dieter Müller and Hansi Müller, were opportunistic pot shots from long range while the Mexicans, again playing poorly, gave them all the room they wanted. For the first 15 minutes only did Mexico offer any real opposition. After that, Hansi Müller, Flohe and Bonhof took control of the midfield and, with the help of Rummenigge and Dieter Müller, brought about the complete collapse of the Mexican defence.

Mexico were certainly not helped by the injury to Pilar-Reyes which obliged them to change their goalkeeper after 38 minutes. But West Germany were 3–0 up by then, and only Cuellar, de la Torre and Hugo Sanchez had resisted West Germany to any great extent. Nor did the replacement of Isiordia with Lopez in attack seem to give them any greater firepower. The same could not be said of West Germany's changes. Their unadventurous formation against Poland reshaped, the world champions were clearly more determined to attack this time. There were, too, odd flashes of the old masterful style. Even so, they were not consistently creative, and one reporter observed that West Germany had tried to derive the maximum benefit from the match with the minimum effort. The 46,000 spectators thoroughly enjoyed themselves, though, and the West Germans left the field to generous applause.

Mexico: Pilar-Reyes (Soto 38 min.), Martinez, Tena, Ramos, Vasquez-Ayala, de la Torre, Cuellar, Mendizabal, Lopez (Lugo 45 min.), Rangel, Sanchez.
West Germany: Maier, Vogts, Rüssmann, Kaltz, Dietz, Bonhof, Flohe (2), H. Müller (1), Rummenigge (2), Fischer, D. Müller (1).
Referee: Farouk Bouzo (Syria).

■ TOP . Hansi Müller beats Pilar—Reyes ■ Leonardo Cuellar races past Rumenigge ■ ABOVE. The one that got away.

MEXICO V POLAND

With this uninspired and uninspiring victory over a much-changed and much-improved Mexican team, Poland won Group Two. No-one expected them to do it, but West Germany were having another of their off-days over at Cordoba against Tunisia at the same time, and these two hard-earned points were sufficient to edge Poland into Group B as winners in the second round. The manner of the victory did not worry Gmoch, Poland's manager. 'We came here to win', he said afterwards. 'We wanted the points, and the rest has no importance'. In other words, Gmoch was simply glad to have killed off the threat from Tunisia – an inconceivable state of affairs at the start – and to have reached the last eight again.

He must have been a worried man for most of the first half because Boniek did not score Poland's first goal until three minutes before the interval. Gmoch could not relax for long, either, because Rangel equalized for Mexico six minutes into the second half, and it was not until seven minutes from the end, when Boniek added a third goal to Deyna's superbly struck goal from outside the box after 56 minutes, that Poland had the game won. Mexico, which introduced five new players – Ortega, Cisneros, Gomez, Flores and Cardenas – simplified their tactics and made many chances.

Cuellar, the brains of their midfield, often threatened to provide the group's second surprising result. No-one was busier than Tomaszewski, the goalkeeper who defied England at Wembley in the 1974 World Cup qualifier. He had to make good saves from Hugo Sanchez, Rangel and Cuellar, and Sanchez and Cuellar also failed in front of goal on other occasions as the Mexicans discovered a new sense of purpose in their final game. It was largely a case of one team having nothing to lose and the other not daring to lose anything.

Poland, which began the game without Nawalka, Szarmach and Lubanski were indebted to the experienced and irrepressible Lato for their victory. Though both he and Deyna were often as uncertain as their colleagues, Lato did make the first two goals. The second one tipped the scales, for it was after that Poland began to get on top and to attack freely, and, as they had qualified for the second round, the Poles could afford to ignore the fact that Mexico, beaten by Tunisia and slaughtered by West Germany, had never really allowed them to settle. Ignore it for the moment, that is.

Mexico: Soto, Flores, Cisneros, Gomez, Vasquez-Ayala, Ortega, de la Torre, Cuellar, Cardenas (Mendizabal 46 min.), Rangel, Sanchez.

Poland: Tomaszewski, Szymanowski, Gorgon, Zmuda, Rudy (Maculewicz 83 min.), Boniek (1), Deyna (2), Kasperczak, Lato, Masztaler, Iwan (Lubanski 75 min.). *Referee*: Jafer Namdar (Iran).

■ The lion-maned Leonardo Cuellar attempts to block a Polish pass.

TUNISIA V W.GERMANY

JUNE 10 CORDOBA GROUP 2   TUNISIA 0 W. GERMANY 0

West Germany ended Group Two as they had begun it, goalless and in disgrace. The crowd of 43,000 – only 3,000 short of a full house at Cordoba's Chateau Carreras Stadium – whistled them off the field at the end, and the Argentinian newspapers castigated them for the technical poverty of their football, their lack of both ideas and a recognizable strategy. West Germany, said *La Nacion,* had no outstanding individuals, no leader and no harmony. It was tempting to believe that the West Germans, always a shrewd World Cup team, had deliberately engineered a draw so that they could go into the group of their choosing, Group A, and stay in Cordoba for the second round. But the final composition of the two second round groups was so uncertain at that point, with more games to come the following day, that the suspicion was easily dismissed. Helmut Schön pointed out too, the risks of playing for a particular result. So one was forced to conclude that West Germany were no longer the force they used to be.

Tunisia might even have beaten them if it had played as aggressively as they had against Mexico and Poland. Instead, obviously a little overawed by the experience of meeting the world champions, the North Africans opted for a defensive posture and the game became bogged down in midfield for long periods. But what they did, they did well. Tunisia's defence was built in an orderly fashion around the gifted Naili, and Dhiab in particular, as well as Lahzami Temime and Gommidh delighted a crowd that warmed to the individual skill of the underdogs. Unquestionably, they carried the affection and appreciation of the world back with them to Tunisia.

Tunisia: Naili, Dhouib, Gommidh, Jebali, Kaabi, Ben Rehaiem, Gasmi, M. Labidi, Dhiab, Lahzami Temime, Akid (R. Ben Aziza 82 min.).

	P	W	D	L	F	A	Pt
POLAND	3	2	1	0	4	1	5
W GERMANY	3	1	2	0	6	0	4
TUNISIA	3	1	1	1	3	2	3
MEXICO	3	0	0	3	2	12	0

West Germany: Maier, Vogts, Rüssmann, Kaltz, Dietz, Bonhof, Flohe, H. Müller, Rummenigge, Fischer, D. Müller.

Referee: Cesar Orozco (Peru).

■ ABOVE. Kaltz faces the determination that earned Tunisia a goalless draw ■ OVER. Torre watches a team mate challenge a Tunisian—without success ■ One minute before Soto's agony ends—Germany score their sixth goal.

GROUP THREE

BRAZIL SWEDEN AUSTRIA SPAIN

Brazil are to the World Cup what air is to breathing – one is unimaginable without the other. The only country to have appeared in all of the 11 World Cup finals and the only one to have won the trophy three times, Brazil hold a special place in the history of the tournament. But such pre-eminence brings with it unique pressures for the man fortunate, or unfortunate, enough to be appointed manager of the national team. To him falls the task of preserving the national heritage: his job is no mere matter of managing a football team, and failure equals the sack more often than not. This is the way of things in a country where the game is more an obsession than a passion.

The situation is complicated further by the inter-state and inter-club rivalries which flourish within Brazilian football and by the absolute conviction of every Brazilian that he is capable of running the national team ten times better than the man appointed to do the job. Joao Saldanha said just that so often and so trenchantly that the Confederacao Brasileira de Desportos (CBD), Brazil's Football Association, invited him to give up journalism again in 1969 and take over their team in the same way as the Botafogo club had done to their benefit 12 years earlier. So Claudio Coutinho could hardly have been unaware of the risks he was running when he accepted the invitation to replace Osvaldo Brandao following the disappointing 0–0 World Cup qualifying result in Colombia in February, 1977.

The glittering individual talents of the immediate Brazilian past, Pele, Tostao, Gerson and Jairzinho, had still not been successfully replaced.

As if the seat were not hot enough in itself, Coutinho brought with him fuel of his own. A physical training instructor in the army in which he held the rank of captain, and a former volleyball player, he was resented from the start because of his military background which prompted some to believe he had been planted in the job deliberately by Brazil's military government. Though, too, he had been coach to the Flamengo club and to the Brazilian amateur team at the 1976 Olympic Games, many more of his fellow countrymen were of the opinion that his sketchy soccer pedigree did not equip him properly for the job of national team manager. Such an unpopular choice was Coutinho, in fact, that even after he had taken Brazil past Colombia, Paraguay, Bolivia and Peru (which had also qualified) into the finals of the World Cup, there was a Press campaign for yet another change of horses in midstream and the recall of Mario Zagalo, Brazil's manager at the 1970 and 1974 finals.

Understandably, then, there was no love lost between Coutinho, who survived for Argentina '78, and the small army which passes for Brazil's newspaper, radio and television reporters. A dark, outrageously good-looking and personable man, he often complained about the demands they made on his time and mental resources ('a two-hour Press conference in the morning, a two-hour Press conference in the afternoon – and always the same questions!'); but his principal objection to the media, he once said, was that they would never allow the manager of Brazil to run the team the way he wanted.

Coutinho's way was to put the emphasis on fitness, stamina and teamwork at the expense of the dazzling, but sometimes self-indulgent, individual skill synonymous with Brazilian football. A great admirer of West Germany and

Holland, he felt that South American football had fallen behind that of Europe and was convinced his synthesis offered Brazil the only means of regaining the world title they had lost in West Germany in 1974. The theory made sense if only because the glittering individual talents of the immediate Brazilian past, Pele, Tostao, Gerson and Jairzinho, had still not been successfully replaced.

Coutinho put it to the test by taking Brazil on an arduous, six-match tour of Europe two months before the 1978 World Cup finals. His critics considered the tour ill-advised, but Coutinho insisted it was necessary to examine thoroughly the capabilities of each member of his squad against European opposition, particularly as Brazil's three rivals in Group Three were Austria, Spain and Sweden. By and large, too, the tour was a success. Though Brazil lost to France and brawled against England, they went home with the psychological advantage of a victory over West Germany and, Coutinho claimed, many new lessons learned.

Resentment still bubbled in Brazil, however, over Coutinho's controversial omission from his World Cup squad of Francisco Marinho, a left back with genuine pretensions to world class, and Paulo Cesar, a left winger of exotic, but erratic skills. While Coutinho explained away the absence of the extrovert pair as a matter of fitness, there were rumblings of discontent, too, from Rivelino, his captain and one remaining star, about the positional play and amount of work expected of him under the new system. So, with Coutinho's attitude to Zico, 'the white Pele', ambivalent as well, Brazil went to Argentina hardly the happiest and most united of the 16 finalists, and yet they went as favourites.

Of their three opponents in the first round group, Spain seemed the most likely to take advantage of Brazil's morale and team selection problems. The determination they had shown by holding off Yugoslavia and Romania in an intensely competitive qualifying group made them a side to be respected, and they were known to have a sound defence built around Pirri, a veteran of the 1966 World Cup – the last in which Spain had competed. The presence of Santillana and the Argentina-born Cano in attack encouraged hopes that the Spaniards would not only concede few goals but score enough to take them into the last eight with Brazil.

As for Sweden, conquerors of Norway and Switzerland at the qualifying stage, they could always be relied on for a spirited contribution to the World Cup. Fourth in 1938, third in 1950, runners-up in 1958 and quarter-finalists in 1974, the Swedes have an enviable record for a small country from which the best players are usually enticed away from Scandinavia by the richer pickings of the European game. With Hellström back in goal, Lennart Larsson playing well in midfield, Edström, their authoritative striker, back in training after injury and a victory over West Germany under their belts, the Swedes looked capable of making their positive presence felt once more.

Brazil were hardly the happiest and most united of the 16 finalists; yet they were favourites.

Austria's prospects were more problematical. They returned to the World Cup finals after an absence of 20 years with a reputation for being less cultured and stylish than in the halcyon days of the Austrian game before and after the last war, but hard to beat. Their 1–0 defeat in Vienna by Holland at the end of May, 1978, for instance, was their first defeat in 15 internationals. They had eliminated East Germany, Turkey and Malta to reach Argentina, and we looked forward with keen anticipation to seeing, among others, Hans Krankl, scorer of six goals in Austria's 9–0 rout of Malta.

SWEDEN V BRAZIL

Only if they had lost to Sweden could Brazil have made a worse start to their 1978 World Cup campaign. A goal down after 38 minutes, Brazil equalized on the stroke of half time; but never at any time did they look either capable or deserving of victory. The worst aspect of a thoroughly poor performance was a disturbing inability to convert scoring chances into goals. Many openings were made in the first half, but only Reinaldo, scorer of the equalizer, appeared likely to find the net. This match will go down in the history of the World Cup as the one in which Clive Thomas, the Welsh referee, denied Brazil a winning goal in the dying seconds. Most were agreed, however, that the Brazilians simply got their just desserts.

The moment of drama came when Brazil forced a corner right at the end. It was taken by Nelinho, who had come on as substitute for Gil 12 minutes from time, and he argued with a linesman over the placing of the ball for the kick. The delay proved costly because, as Nelinho's kick was in the air, Thomas blew the final whistle. So Zico's scoring header was too late, his celebration in the Swedish net mere pantomime, and Sweden walked off a pitch that had cut up badly with a point they fully merited. No amount of Brazilian wailing and gnashing of teeth could drown out the truth of the matter.

Living up to their World Cup tradition, Sweden were a difficult handful. They played with the self-confidence of a team that chose to ignore the fact that Brazil were former world champions, and they found no difficulty in stopping or attacking their illustrious opponents. Simple, practical, direct and quick-thinking, the Swedes took the lead with a very good goal. Wendt and Linderoth played their parts before Lennart Larsson gave Sjoberg the opportunity to beat Leao with a firm, right-foot shot. Wendt, too, was most unlucky soon afterwards when he hit the bar after beating both Oscar and Amaral, Brazil's formidable central defenders.

Reinaldo brought Brazil level when a Cerezo centre caused a misunderstanding between two Swedish defenders, but the goal did nothing to make them any more convincing. Their lack of personality, leadership and rhythm were painfully apparent, and the late substitutions of Nelinho for Gil and of Dirceu for Cerezo effected little improvement. Nor did Edström set the world on fire when he came on for Lennart Larsson during the same period. Nevertheless, this was still a triumph for little Sweden, a minor disaster for Brazil.

The match was also notable in that the 35-year old Swedish captain, Bjorn Nordqvist, was playing in his 109th international and, in the process, breaking the world record held by England's Bobby Moore.

Sweden: Hellström, Borg, Roy Andersson, Nordqvist, Erlandsson, B. Larsson, Tapper, L. Larsson (Edström 79 min.), Linderoth, Wendt, Sjoberg (1).

Brazil: Leao, Toninho, Oscar, Amaral, Edinho, Batista, Cerezo (Dirceu 80 min.), Rivelino, Gil (Nelinho 78 min.), Zico, Reinaldo (1).

Referee: Clive Thomas (Wales).

SPAIN V AUSTRIA

While Brazil were stumbling along at Mar Del Plata, Austria quickly got into full stride at the smaller of Buenos Aires' two World Cup grounds. Better organized and more disciplined tactically than Spain, Austria claimed an opening victory that, for all its narrowness, was clear enough. Though the prolific Krankl did not score his side's winning goal until the 79th minute, the triumph of Austrian order over Spanish emotion was obvious long before. In a rather confused match played at great pace, all the clarity was provided by the Austrians.

Spain began promisingly enough, but they could not overcome an Austrian team strong in defence, ordered in midfield and dangerous in attack. Pezzey's elegant forays upfield, the dribbling of Prohaska and Kreuz and the searching runs of Krankl and Schachner presented Spain with a series of difficult problems. It was Schachner who opened the scoring after only two minutes, and Miguel Angel had to save well from Jara before Dani equalized with a deflected shot in the 21st minute. Cano had a 'goal' disallowed shortly before half time, but Spain lost all chance of getting on top when their manager, Ladislao Kubala, made a mystifying substitution during the interval.

For some reason best known to himself, Kubala chose to withdraw Cardenosa, generally regarded as Spain's most able player during the first half, and replace him with the inferior Leal. The change threw a greater burden than ever on Marcelino, San Jose, Asensi and Rexach, and they finally collapsed under its weight when, with both teams apparently settling for a draw, Kreuz suddenly burst forward and Krankl lost Migueli to score the winner.

Spain: Miguel Angel, Marcelino, Pirri, Migueli, De la Cruz, San Jose, Asensi, Cardenosa (Leal 46 min.), Dani (1), Cano, Rexach (Quini 60 min.).
Austria: Koncilia, Sara, Obermayer, Pezzey, Breitenberger, Prohaska, Hickersberger (Weber 67 min.), Kreuz, Jara, Schachner (1) (Pirkner 80 min.), Krankl (1).
Referee: Karoly Palotai (Hungary).

■ OPPOSITE. Amaral beats Sjoberg in the air ■ ABOVE. A Spanish attempt is covered by Hickersberger and Koncilia.

BRAZIL V SPAIN

JUNE 7 MAR DEL PLATA GROUP 3   BRAZIL 0 SPAIN 0

It was after this second, disappointing draw the story went around that Claudio Coutinho had been sacked as manager of Brazil. The rumour proved to be just that, but Coutinho stayed on in a reduced capacity and his effigy was burned in the streets of Rio de Janeiro. Convinced that Brazil were not going to qualify for the second round, one devoted Brazilian fan even went so far as to commit suicide by drinking insecticide. His despair was a trifle premature as it turned out, but no-one was to know that as Brazil continued to stumble.

This certainly was an unsatisfactory point, miserably gained. Coutinho complained afterwards about the heavy, spongy pitch. It, he said, affected Brazil more than the Europeans because a change of pace was central to the Brazilian style of play. But most observers concluded that Coutinho was simply making excuses for Brazil's palpable inability to overcome any side which confronted them with a well-organized defence. Without Rivelino, who was said to have damaged an ankle in the second half against Sweden, Brazil lacked authority in midfield. There was, too, a shortage of power and width in attack, where Reinaldo was left isolated and forlorn.

Zico and Dirceu showed occasional flashes of inspiration, but Coutinho's gamble of dropping Gil, his right winger, and playing Toninho, an attacking

full back, wide on the right was a total failure. Nelinho, Toninho's replacement, fired in shots from all distances and angles without troubling Miguel Angel more than once, and the Spanish goalkeeper was beaten on only one occasion throughout. That was when Olmo, one of his own defenders, headed against the underside of Spain's crossbar while under pressure from Zico during the first half. Indeed, Spain benefited considerably from the five changes they made in the team beaten 2–1 by Austria.

Two of them were caused by injury, but another, the introduction of Real Madrid's Santillana for the Argentina-born Cano in attack was forced upon Kubala, the manager, by 'player power'.

In the event, the latter nearly proved decisive because it was Santillana who headed down Uria's long, high ball to give Cardenosa the best scoring chance of the game 15 minutes from the end. Sadly, because he had again been Spain's outstanding player, Cardenosa shot weakly enough for Amaral to be able to clear the ball off the goal line.

Brazil: Leao, Nelinho (Gil 69 min.), Oscar, Amaral, Edinho, Cerezo, Batista, Dirceu, Toninho, Reinaldo, Zico (Mendonca 84 min.).

Spain: Miguel Angel, Marcelino, Migueli (Biosca 50 min.), Uria (Guzman 78 min.), Olmo, San Jose, Leal, Asensi, Juanito, Santillana, Cardenosa.

Referee: Sergio Gonella (Italy).

■ TOP. Edinho falls heavily ■ Spain defend desperately against Reinaldo and Zico

AUSTRIA V SWEDEN

Austria maintained their promising first match form here, but the move from Mar Del Plata seemed to have drained Sweden of most of the enterprise they had shown against Brazil. Even though the goal that assured them of a place in the last eight was scored from a dubious penalty, Austria were worthy winners. All the brightest attacking ideas were theirs, and Sweden did little more than huddle protectively around Hellström whenever they lost the ball, which was frequently. In a tediously lethargic first half, particularly, the Swedes seemed interested only in avoiding defeat.

Austria mounted most of the rare attacks in that first 45 minutes. Hellström, Sweden's busiest and most able player on the day, had to save well from Krankl twice and also turn a Kreuz header for a corner before the thrusting Krankl forced the penalty from which he won the game for Austria three minutes before the interval. The kick was awarded when Krankl pushed the ball past Nordqvist, Sweden's captain, and fell to the ground as he attempted to dart after it. A deliberate dive over Nordqvist's legs was suspected by some, but the referee ruled that Krankl had been tripped.

Only in the second half did Sweden relax their defensive posture. They did so in response to Krankl's goal and to Austria's obvious intention of preserving their lead and conserving their energies with controlled, possession football. Even then, Prohaska and Jara exploited the gaps the advancing Swedes left behind them, and control of the midfield was soon Austria's once more. Krankl began to harry Sweden on both flanks and Hellström had to excel himself to prevent Austria scoring on six occasions. Sweden's last, desperate throw was to introduce Edström half an hour from the end, but they were never able to exploit his height. So Austria moved into the second round with something to spare, and that shrewd tactician, Helmut Senekowitsch, was confirmed as the most successful manager of Austria since he himself had been an international player 20 years earlier.

Austria: Koncilia, Sara, Pezzey, Obermayer, Breitenberger, Prohaska, Hickersberger, Kreuz, Kreiger (Weber 71 min.), Krankl (1), Jara.

Sweden: Hellström, Erlandsson, Nordqvist, Roy Andersson, Borg, Tapper (Torstensson 36 min.), Linderoth (Edström 60 min.), L. Larsson, B. Larsson, Sjoberg, Wendt.

Referee: Charles Corver (Holland).

■ ABOVE. Krankl aims a volley.

AUSTRIA V BRAZIL

JUNE 11 MAR DEL PLATA GROUP 3   AUSTRIA 0 BRAZIL 1

The situation on this tense, chilly Sunday afternoon was quite simple: having drawn with Sweden and Spain, Brazil, 9–4 favourites to win the 1978 World Cup before it started, had to beat Austria, unexpected leaders of Group Three, to ensure qualification for the second round and the avoidance of national disgrace. The background, however, was more complicated. While it had become clear that Claudio Coutinho had not been removed from his post as first thought, it was not known exactly how much power he had lost to the officials in charge of the Brazilian delegation. Its head, Admiral Heleno Nunez, was said to have thrown his weight about to such effect that a five-man selection committee had been set up to monitor Coutinho's choice of players.

Whoever was responsible, Brazil made four changes. One of them was unavoidable, since Nelinho had been injured against Spain, but not the others. Zico, Reinaldo and Edinho were all dropped and Mendonca, Roberto, Rodrigues Neto and Gil brought in to fill the four vacancies. The omission of Zico and Reinaldo from the attack was the most radical alteration because those two slight, gifted youngsters had been regarded as the players most likely to pick up the torch of Brazilian football dropped by Pele and Tostao. Coutinho explained afterwards that Mendonca and Roberto had been preferred because their greater physical strength was better suited to the difficult Mar Del Plata pitch. Nevertheless, there was no mistaking the desperation in the Brazilian camp as they prepared to risk all against Austria.

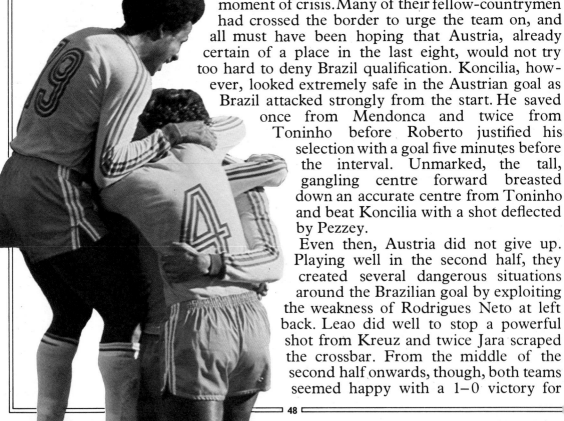

Brazil certainly did not lack support in their moment of crisis. Many of their fellow-countrymen had crossed the border to urge the team on, and all must have been hoping that Austria, already certain of a place in the last eight, would not try too hard to deny Brazil qualification. Koncilia, however, looked extremely safe in the Austrian goal as Brazil attacked strongly from the start. He saved once from Mendonca and twice from Toninho before Roberto justified his selection with a goal five minutes before the interval. Unmarked, the tall, gangling centre forward breasted down an accurate centre from Toninho and beat Koncilia with a shot deflected by Pezzey.

Even then, Austria did not give up. Playing well in the second half, they created several dangerous situations around the Brazilian goal by exploiting the weakness of Rodrigues Neto at left back. Leao did well to stop a powerful shot from Kreuz and twice Jara scraped the crossbar. From the middle of the second half onwards, though, both teams seemed happy with a 1–0 victory for

Brazil because it would mean qualification for them both. Neither wanted to waste energy unnecessarily and the game subsided into a boring exhibition of possession football. There was encouragement for Brazil, however, in the form of Dirceu in midfield and of Oscar and Amaral at the heart of the defence. Afterwards, Coutinho said prophetically: 'We marked efficiently and managed to attack often. We have gained in force as a team. . . . We have a better defence than in 1970 and 1974, and only now, in the second round, will we play as well as we expect.'

Brazil: Leao, Toninho, Oscar, Amaral, Rodrigues Neto, Cerezo (Chicao 71 min.), Batista, Dirceu, Gil, Roberto (1), Mendonca (Zico 84 min.).
Austria: Koncilia, Sara, Obermayer, Pezzey, Breitenberger, Prohaska, Hickersberger (Weber 61 min.), Jara, Kreuz, Krankl, Kreiger (Happich 84 min.).
Referee: Robert Wurtz (France).

OPPOSITE. Mendonca and Amaral join in celebrating Roberto's goal ■ ABOVE TOP. Gil avoids Kreiger's tackle INSET. Neto bursts through between Pezzey and Hickersberger ■ Cerezo, Batista and Amaral watch Roberto's free kick as Kreuz, Kreiger, Prohaska, Hickersberger and Pezzey crowd and cower round another Brazilian.

SWEDEN V SPAIN

JUNE 11 BUENOS AIRES GROUP 3   SWEDEN 0 SPAIN 1

Sweden just about gave up the ghost in their final Group Three match, but not Spain. Conscious that victory here could take them into the last eight if Brazil failed to beat Austria the same afternoon, Spain dominated this game completely. The scoreline flattered Sweden because Spain created a host of scoring chances without being able to take more than one of them. The reason was a combination of poor finishing by the Spaniards and another excellent display of goalkeeping by the consistent Hellström. Even he was powerless in the 76th minute, however, when Juanito made an opening for Asensi, who outpaced both of Sweden's central defenders to drive a left-foot shot into Sweden's net. Juanito played upfield on his own in a curious 4–5–1 formation that looked to be ultra-defensive to start with. But Uria, Asensi and Cardenosa soon dispelled that notion by launching a series of attacks that gave the Swedish defence a lot of trouble. Edström played his first full game for Sweden, but renewed attempts to exploit his heading ability were thwarted by the tight marking of Marcelino. Sweden did trouble the Spanish defence occasionally with high centres, but the introduction of Pirri for the second half stiffened their resistance noticeably.

Sweden: Hellström, Borg, Roy Andersson, Nordqvist, Erlandsson, Nordin, Nilsson, B. Larsson, L. Larsson, Sjoberg (Linderoth 66 min.), Edström (Wendt 59 min.).

Spain: Miguel Angel, Marcelino, Olmo (Pirri 46 min.), Biosca, Uria, Leal, Cardenosa, Asensi (1), Santillana, San Jose, Juanito.

Referee: Ferdinand Biwersi (West Germany).

	P	W	D	L	F	A	Pt
AUSTRIA	3	2	0	1	3	2	4
BRAZIL	3	1	2	0	2	1	4
SPAIN	3	1	1	1	2	2	3
SWEDEN	3	0	1	2	1	3	1

■ Another excellent display of skill from Ronnie Hellström but even he could not save Asensi's shot.

GROUP FOUR

HOLLAND SCOTLAND PERU IRAN

None of the 16 finalists could have gone to Argentina with more self-confidence than Scotland. This confidence was not entirely justified because the Scots had failed to win a match in the British Championship, including having lost at home to England in their final fixture before the World Cup finals. But the setbacks were pushed to one side as some 30,000 loyalists turned up at Hampden Park in midweek to give their heroes a rousing sendoff. At the same time, the managers of several other finalists were continuing to tip Scotland as the team most likely to cause a surprise in Argentina. The wave of euphoria was further enlarged by the opinion of a number of respected judges that the 22 players about to cross the Atlantic comprised the best Scotland team ever.

That optimistic assessment was based largely on the difficulty Ally MacLeod, Scotland's new manager, had had in whittling down to 22 his original squad of 40 players. Never, it seemed, had Scotland been blessed with more talent and alternatives in every position on the field. So deep were their resources that

"Of course we'll win the World Cup. If I say that, it saves you from asking me the question again"—Macleod.

even the early withdrawal of Danny McGrain, Celtic's seasoned and world-class full back, because of injury and the knee damage suffered by Gordon McQueen, the first choice centre half, on the eve of departure were seen as opportunities for other players rather than as the crippling losses they were to become. After all, Scottish thinking went, they were in a weak group with Peru and Iran, and that meant they were certain to qualify with Holland for the last eight.

Scotland had appeared in the World Cup finals three times before, but had never succeeded in reaching the last eight. In fact, they had only ever won one game – against Zaire in 1974. This time, though, it was going to be different. The only possible impediment to steady Scottish progress in Argentina, most people decided, would be the fiery temperament of the players. Several of them, it was feared, were quite likely to lose their heads in the heat of battle and run the risk of being sent off. MacLeod himself was aware of this danger, but pointed out, quite reasonably, that the Scottish footballer was nothing without his fighting spirit. As it happens, no other answer was possible from a man whose stock-in-trade was fire and brimstone.

A self-confessed extrovert, MacLeod had climbed the managerial ladder with Ayr United and Aberdeen impressively enough to be taken on by the Scottish Football Association as successor to the reticent Willie Ormond, whose Scotland team had departed unbeaten from the 1974 World Cup. He relinquished the job and its pressures in May, 1977 in order to return to Scottish club football with the Edinburgh side, Hearts. As MacLeod said at the time: 'Willie Ormond and I are like chalk and cheese. He's an introvert and I'm an extrovert.' MacLeod was definitely a manager who led from the front, and the Scottish public loved his rousing battle cries ('Of course we'll win the World Cup. If I say that, it saves you asking me the question again.') as much as the SFA relished his ability to beguile the Scottish Press. There was talk of a breath of fresh air

Group Four

blowing through the dusty corridors of Scottish football power, and there seemed no limit to where MacLeod's mouth could take Scotland after the elimination of Czechoslovakia, the European champions, and stubborn Wales.

Those who had not fallen under MacLeod's spell did have certain misgivings about Scotland's prospects. There was, for instance, concern about both MacLeod's last-minute experiments with the team in the British Championship and his refusal to include Andy Gray, a proven goalscorer in the hard world of English football, in his final squad. Even so, Scotland still appeared to have enough good players and sufficient self-belief to dismiss Peru and Iran. Peru were dismissed as a fragile bunch of ageing ball players because the survival of many of the team that had reached the quarter finals in 1970 gave them the oldest squad in Argentina. Conveniently ignored was the fact that only Brazil had managed to beat Peru during the tortuous South American qualifying process. It should have been a warning to Scotland, too, that the Peruvians had been in full training since the beginning of the year under Marcos Calderon, their thickset and perceptive manager.

Iran's presence in Argentina was a tribute to the groundwork done for them by Frank O'Farrell, the Irishman who left club football in England to establish the Iranian national team on a sound footing. His successor, Heshmat Mohajerani, carried on from where O'Farrell left off with such success that

Happel—A prickly character with a lugubrious face evoking memories of comedian Tony Hancock.

Iran overcame, among others, Australia, qualifiers in 1974, and Kuwait, managed by Brazil's Mario Zagalo, to reach Argentina. Rowshan and Parvin were said to be useful players, but the Iranians looked to have nothing like the pace or strength to disturb a European side.

MacLeod was certain that the Cup itself would be won by a European side, but while he had a sneaking regard for Hungary, most others would have plumped for Holland as the side most likely to break Europe's duck in South America. Though Cruyff had gone, and Van Hanegem, too, Holland could still call on nine of the players who had appeared in the final of the 1974 World Cup – ten if you counted Rene Van der Kerkhof's appearance as substitute. Van Hanegem's late withdrawal had settled the argument over whether he or Rensenbrink should become the team's central figure in succession to Cruyff, but there was still enough bickering going on to indicate that the Dutch were approaching Argentina in the disorganized way that suited only them.

In place of the legendary Rinus Michels, inventor of the so-called 'total football' of 1974, Holland had the former Austrian international, Ernst Happel, as their manager. A prickly character with a lugubrious face evoking memories of comedian Tony Hancock, Happel had proved himself a sound tactician by taking Bruges, the Belgian champions, into the final of the 1978 European Cup. He tended to stand aloof from the players while Jan Zwartkruis, his much friendlier assistant, acted as go-between. Zwartkruis, an officer in the Dutch Air Force, had been in charge of Holland the night they had overwhelmed Don Revie's England with an absolutely brilliant performance to win 2–0 at Wembley in February, 1977. The same standard had not been attained while Holland were eliminating Belgium, Northern Ireland and Iceland, but their improved form in a Paris tournament and in beating Austria in Vienna just before the World Cup finals suggested they were coming to a peak again at the right time.

PERU V SCOTLAND

To the horror and stunned disbelief of the 700 or so Scottish fans who had trekked to Argentina from all parts of the globe, Scotland were virtually out of the 1978 World Cup almost before it had started. This totally unexpected defeat in their opening match meant that Scotland had to beat both Iran and Holland to retain any chance of reaching the second round. But few would have backed the Scots to do so on the evidence of their abject capitulation to Peru after taking an early lead and dominating the first 15 minutes of the game so completely.

] The agony and the anger in Cordoba □ LEFT. Masson starts his run. Quiroga moves. Off balance Masson kicks □ The ball is hit o soft and too close to Quiroga □ RIGHT. Quiroga saves □ Quiroga, El Loco, roars his joy □ BOTTOM LEFT. Dalglish loots, but misses □ BOTTOM RIGHT. Jordan celebrates the goal □ ABOVE. Two angry Scots amuse the Argentinians.

Though Donachie was suspended and McQueen injured, this was basically the team that had taken Scotland to Argentina and the one that had lost undeservedly to England just before departure. MacLeod's questionable reliance on the partnership of Rioch, Masson and Hartford in midfield looked to have been justified as the three of them drove forward eagerly from the start. Masson and Hartford both got through Peru's predictably sketchy defence for shots at Quiroga before a first-time drive by Rioch opened the way for Scotland's goal after 14 minutes. Quiroga could not hold Rioch's blast, and Jordan gleefully steered the loose ball into an empty net.

Jordan had been expected to terrorize the suspect Peruvian defence with his power in the air and general aggression. So when Velasquez was booked for fouling the Scottish striker for the second time in the first 19 minutes, it looked

■ The beginning and the end ■ TOP. Scottish fans celebrate, briefly ■ BOTTOM. Nine Peruvians celebrate Cubillas' second goal ■ OVER. Forsyth and Hartford congratulate a rampant Jordan ■ The scoreboard records Peru's third goal.

Peru V Scotland

as though Jordan's mission was having some success. At that point, however, Cubillas decided it was time to show what a genuine world-class player could do. Aided by Cueto in midfield, the former winger pushed Peru forward to attack Scotland with dazzling short passes through the middle or with centres and shots from Munante and Oblitas, a pair of tricky, speedy wingers.

One crisis followed another in the Scottish goalmouth. Yet Dalglish could have scored twice from passes by Jordan before Peru equalized three minutes before the interval, Cueto applying the final touch to a devastating burst of one-twos through the middle of a bemused Scottish defence. Peru continued to dictate the pace at the start of the second half, but Scotland gradually began to come forward again and the referee, somewhat generously, awarded them a penalty after 64 minutes when Rioch was brought down by Cubillas. Masson, Scotland's penalty expert, took the kick but succeeded only in giving Quiroga a soft shot to save. That was Scotland's last chance. Peru overran them in the final 25 minutes and Cubillas, the game's outstanding player, beat Rough with two blinding shots, one a free kick, in the 70th and 77th minutes.

Afterwards, MacLeod blamed his players for the defeat, 'The sort of thing that happened today is the bane of a manager's life. We played for 15 minutes, got one up and needed to play for just another 15 minutes. Then the game would have been over. But suddenly they got all casual when all they had to do was keep finding Jordan. I don't know what came over them. This is football – I don't know what happens to players when they get into these sort of moods. . . . There are no easy games in the World Cup.'

Peru: Quiroga, Duarte, Manzo, Chumpitaz, Diaz, Velasquez, Cubillas (2), Cueto (1) (P. Rojas 82 min.), Munante, La Rosa (Sotil 62 min.), Oblitas.

Scotland: Rough, Kennedy, Forsyth, Burns, Buchan, Rioch (Macari 70 min.), Masson (Gemmill 70 min.), Hartford, Jordan (1), Dalglish, Johnston.

Referee: Ulf Eriksson (Sweden).

Gemmill dejected, his twenty minutes of effort unrewarded

Peru V Scotland

SEIKO   CRONOMETRO OFICIAL

PERIODO

TIEMPO DE JUEGO

STEWART – WARNE   AUTOTROL

HOLLAND V IRAN

JUNE 3 MENDOZA GROUP 4   HOLLAND 3 IRAN 0

While Scotland were being tumbled by Peru, Holland were having traumas of their own against the least-fancied side in the Group. Iran had come to Argentina with a reputation for being well-organized, but until they stretched the 1974 runners-up no-one really believed their organization was sufficiently ironclad to protect them against the wiles of European and South American football. Holland, it must be said, were a mere shadow of the side that captivated the world four years earlier. Without Cruyff, they lacked for a long time the inspiration.and imagination needed to unlock a steely Iranian defence. Yet, to emphasize Holland's faults would have been less than justice to World Cup novices who occasionally carried the game to the Dutch dangerously.

In fact, Iran very nearly scored first after 8 minutes, Faraki's shot taking a deflection off Rijsbergen and rolling the wrong side of a post with Jongbloed out of position. With Parvin, making his 80th appearance for his country, and Nazari giving Iran momentum, Holland were made to look quite ordinary at

times. Rep, Rensenbrink and Neeskens displayed few of their world-class gifts, and Holland struggled to penetrate the Iranian fortress until the 38th minute, when Rene Van der Kerkhof was brought down in the penalty area by Abdollahi. Rensenbrink sent Hejazi the wrong way with his spot kick and Holland could begin to breath a little more easily.

Rensenbrink, who headed the second goal at the far post from a centre in the 62nd minute, completed the first hat-trick of the 1978 World Cup and achieved the distinction of becoming the 17th player to score three times in a World Cup match when he converted another penalty 13 minutes from the end. By then, Holland were beginning to show what a force they could be. Overall, however, it had been an unconvincing start by one of the sides tipped to go far in the finals.

Iran: Hejazi, Nazari, Abdollahi, Kazerani, Eskandarjan, Parvin, Ghasimpour, Sadeghi, Naibagha, Jahani, Faraki (Rowshan 50 min.).

Holland: Jongbloed, Suurbier, Krol, Rijsbergen, Neeskens, Haan, Jansen, W. Van der Kerkhof, Rep, Rensenbrink (3), R. Van der Kerkhof (Nanninga 70 min.).

Referee: Alfonso Archundia (Mexico).

■ Rob Rensenbrink scored the first hat-trick of Argentina '78, but failed to show his many other skills.

SCOTLAND V IRAN

JUNE 7 CORDOBA GROUP 4   SCOTLAND 1 IRAN 1

By the time they returned to the Chateau Carreras Stadium four days after their defeat by Peru, Scotland were in disgrace. The random dope test which follows every World Cup match had singled out Scotland's Willie Johnston and Kenny Dalglish, with positive results in Johnston's case. The West Bromwich Albion winger was found guilty of taking a stimulant, fencamfamin, rated highly dangerous by FIFA, and the Scottish officials had little option but to send him home and ban him for life. While Johnston's performance against Peru had been lethargic enough to give stimulants a bad name, he could console himself with the thought that he, at least, had been spared any association with this subsequent truly appalling Scotland performance.

■ ABOVE. Jordan keeps trying and trying and trying and trying and...

Scotland V Iran

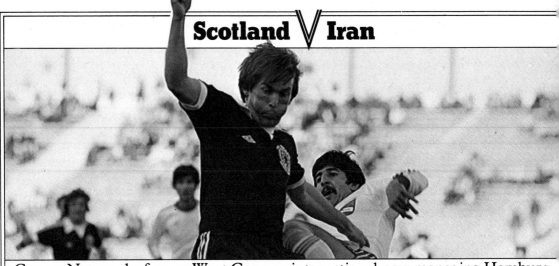

Gunter Netzer, the former West German international now managing Hamburg, emerged from the stands at the end shaking his head in bewilderment. 'I have seen it,' he said, 'but I don't believe it.' What he had seen was Scotland play worse than Iran and struggle to hold them to a draw. In fact, the Scots did not score themselves in this game. They were saved from defeat by the own goal Eskandarjan inadvertently steered past Hejazi shortly before halftime. Danalfar equalized on the hour when Scotland were guilty of four or five defensive errors in succession as Parvin put Sadeghi away on the right for a centre, and Ghasimpour should have settled it two minutes later by doing better with Faraki's lovely through pass than run it straight into goalkeeper Rough's possession.

MacLeod made a total of six changes in the side beaten by Peru. The full back pairing of Kennedy and Buchan was broken up after their roasting by Munante and Oblitas, Kennedy losing his place and Buchan being restored to his normal position of sweeper at the expense of Forsyth. Gemmill and Macari were preferred to the men they had replaced late in the game against Peru – Masson and Rioch – and Robertson was brought in to replace Johnston on the left wing. Though many continued to lament the absence of Souness from midfield and of Derek Johnstone from the attack, most of the alterations made some sense. Yet nothing happened. Scotland, even clumsier and more inept than they had been against Peru, managed to make the novices of Iran look world-beaters.

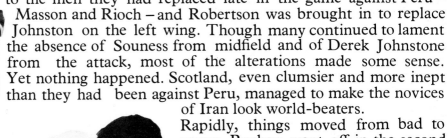

Rapidly, things moved from bad to worse. Buchan went off in the second half with blood flowing from his face after a wound which had been inflicted not by an opponent but by his own full back, Donachie, who accidentally kicked the Manchester United player in the face as he tried to head a bouncing ball. Buchan took with him most of the coherence in Scotland's football, and it was not until the portly Harper replaced Dalglish, out of touch again in a World Cup, in the last quarter of an hour that Scotland began to move

Scotland V Iran

with some urgency although little rhythm. But by then, of course, it was too late. This time, it was an extremely subdued Ally MacLeod who accompanied his captain for the day, Archie Gemmill, to the post-match Press conference. The man who had trumpeted after the Peru defeat, 'It's the Battle of Bannockburn over the next two games', now admitted quietly, 'We didn't play at all. We have been under some pressure, but we knew we had to win to stay in. Individually and collectively we did not play well. Overall it was a poor performance.' So poor did the watching Scottish supporters think it had been, that they surrounded the Scotland team bus as it prepared to leave the ground and vented their feelings by rocking the vehicle from side to side and screaming insults at the players and officials.

Scotland: Rough, Jardine, Burns, Buchan (Forsyth 56 min.), Donachie, Gemmill, Macari, Hartford, Jordan, Dalglish (Harper 74 min.), Robertson.

Iran: Hejazi, Nazari, Abdollahi, Kazerani, Eskandarjan (o.g.), Parvin, Ghasimpour, Sadeghi, Danalfar (1), Faraki, Jahani.

Referee: Youssou N'Diaye (Senegal).

■ OPPOSITE TOP. Dalglish bursts through Iran's defence ■ Gemmill's efforts take him clean over Sadeghi's back
■ ABOVE. Hejazi shows his feelings over the own goal ■ Iran confidently leave space behind them as they attack
■ '6,000 miles for this rubbish!'

HOLLAND V PERU

Alerted to Peru's attacking potential by their runaway victory over Scotland, Happel, Holland's manager, opted for the cautious approach in this game. Having tried a 3–4–3 formation against Iran, Happel dropped Rep from the attack, brought in Poortvliet, a versatile youngster, and packed his midfield in an attempt to smother at birth Peru's thrusts through the middle and down the flanks. The success of Holland's redeployment into 3–5–2 can be judged by the scoreline and by the fact that Peru troubled Jongbloed seriously only once in the first half and then during the last 10 minutes of the game. Happel's pragmatism was undoubtedly effective, yet it was sad to see a side which had built its reputation on fluid, attacking football reduced to such negative thinking.

Once again the absence of Cruyff was underlined heavily. Peru, the team least capable of offering stout defensive resistance, coped easily with Holland's slow deliberate attacks mounted from midfield, and the eccentric Quiroga was put under pressure only occasionally. He made his best save low to his left to stop a left-foot shot from Rensenbrink, the only Dutchman who showed any real appetite or aptitude for scoring. Holland deteriorated as the game grew older. The substitutions of Rep and Nanninga for Rene Van der Kerkhof and the injured Neeskens effected little improvement and the Dutch ended the match defending themselves against a series of the Cubillas free kicks which had undone Scotland.

Holland: Jongbloed, Suurbier, Krol, Rijsbergen, Neeskens (Nanninga 67 min.), Haan, Jansen, W. Van der Kerkhof, Poortvliet, R. Van der Kerkhof (Rep 46 min.), Rensenbrink.

Peru: Quiroga, Duarte, Manzo, Chumpitaz, Diaz, Velasquez, Cubillas, Cueto, Munante, La Rosa (Sotil 63 min.), Oblitas.

Referee: Adolf Prokop (East Germany).

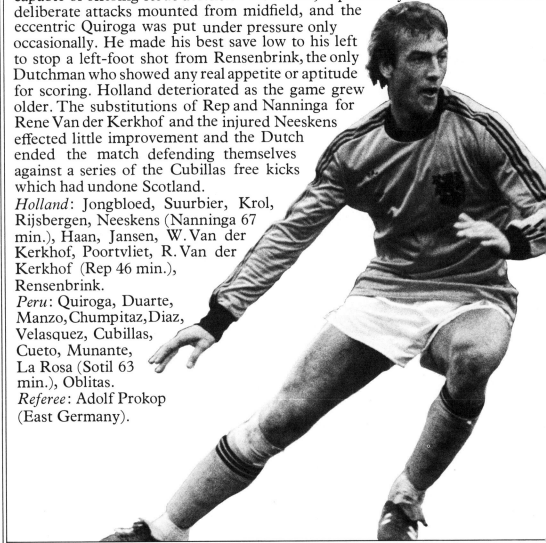

■ Johan Neeskens, Hollands midfield dynamo sustained injury and was later substituted.

PERU V IRAN

Peru won Group Four and qualified for the second round in the flamboyant attacking style to which we had been accustomed. Three goals by the 29 year old Cubillas, two of them penalties, found the Iranian defence vulnerable to typical South American football played at speed and with accuracy, but the Iranians fought to the last and often exposed the chronic weakness of the Peruvian defence, particularly in the air.

In truth, though, Iran never really recovered from the shock of finding themselves a goal down after two minutes, when Velasquez scored with a spectacular header. Peru dominated the game almost totally from then on.

Yet Iran might have scored themselves before Peru's lightning one-twos paid real dividends. A superb through ball from Kazerani split the Peruvian defence, and only Quiroga's agility prevented Rowshan from scoring with a right foot shot after 29 minutes. It was Iran's best chance in a match that ran away from them when Peru were awarded a dubious penalty in the 35th minute for a foul on Oblitas at the edge of the area. Cubillas put that one away, and then made no mistake with Peru's second penalty three minutes later when he himself was brought down by Hejazi.

The persistent Rowshan dragged Iran back into the game with a goal five minutes before half time, and the Iranians went on the offensive early in the second half without being able to reduce the deficit further. As Peru took over once more, Munante got the ball into the net only to find that Oblitas had been penalized for a foul on Hejazi.

Then, with 12 minutes left to play, Cubillas applied the *coup de grâce* by beating two defenders and flicking the ball under Hejazi.

Peru: Quiroga, Duarte, Manzo (Leguia 67 min.), Chumpitaz, Diaz, Velasquez (1), Cubillas (3), Cueto, Munante, La Rosa (Sotil 60 min.), Oblitas.

Iran: Hejazi, Nazari, Abdollahi, Kazerani, Allahvardi, Danalfar, Parvin, Sadeghi, Ghasimpour, Rowshan (1) (Fariba 66 min.), Faraki (Jahani 51 min.).

Referee: Alojzy Jarguz (Poland).

■ Teofilo Cubillas applied the coup de grâce.

HOLLAND V SCOTLAND

JUNE 11 MENDOZA GROUP 4 HOLLAND 2 SCOTLAND 3

'Miracles do happen,' Ally Macleod had said without enthusiasm while discussing Scotland's chances of beating Holland by three clear goals – the margin needed to squeeze the Scots into the second round. But he was so nearly right. When, after 68 minutes, Archie Gemmill dribbled right through the Dutch defence to put Scotland 3–1 up with what *El Grafico,* the Argentinian sports magazine, believed to be the best goal of the tournament, Scottish reporters were on their feet in the Press box punching the air and their noisy compatriots on the terraces, so angry only a few days earlier, were preparing to forgive and forget. Only one more goal and Scotland would have achieved the impossible.

■ The miracle almost happened ■ BLUE. Gemmill scores the third goal and Scots all round the world rejoice ■ ABOVE AND OPPOSITE. Souness and Gemmill almost made it possible ■ Souness is upended and Gemmill scores Scotland's second goal from the penalty.

Holland V Scotland

That, however, was the closest they were to come to the last eight. Four minutes later, Johnny Rep was allowed to run unmarked from midfield and drill the ball into the top corner of the net from 25 yards. Rough got a hand to the shot, but it must have been like trying to stop a guided missile. As Scotland went down like a burst balloon, Holland nearly scored again, Rene Van der Kerkhof catching Rough out with a shot that went under the goalkeeper's body and past the far post. One desperate header by Forsyth later Scotland were out of the World Cup on their customary high note while Holland sneaked into the second round on goal difference.

Any resemblance between this Scottish performance and those against Peru and Iran was purely coincidental. Here, in the foothills of the Andes, Scotland's football was suddenly as crisp and clear as the mountain air. All the fuzziness and lethargy of the Cordoban dustbowl disappeared as if by magic. But the real reason can be attributed simply to MacLeod's first attack of commonsense. By at last picking Graeme Souness and by recalling Rioch, Forsyth and Kennedy, Scotland's manager belatedly discovered the right blend of players.

Recapturing at once his form for Liverpool in their successful defence of the European Cup, Souness imposed his will on the game with a stream of imaginative and accurate passes. He was in his element because Scotland had regrouped in a 4-4-2 formation like Liverpool's and Souness specializes in finding men going forward from midfield into scoring positions. Dalglish looked a different player entirely as Souness, his teammate at Liverpool, plied him with the sort of passes he could use. It was no coincidence, therefore, when Dalglish volleyed Scotland's equalizer from a Jordan header made possible by Souness' deep centre in the 44th minute.

Holland had taken the lead ten minutes earlier with another of Rensenbrink's many penalties in the tournament. Nothing could have been more cruel to Scotland. Apart from the fact that Kennedy was penalized for what appeared to be a perfectly legitimate retrieving tackle on Rep, the spot kick Rensenbrink clipped past Rough turned out to be a World Cup milestone – its 1000th goal. Since Rioch had already headed a Souness centre against the bar and Dalglish had been refused what looked to be a perfectly good goal from a chip shot, Holland hardly deserved the honour of bringing up the thousand. Having lost the injured Neeskens early in the first half, and having chosen the wrong tactics, the Dutch were in tatters throughout the first half.

To his credit, Ernst Happel rectified his error of setting Suurbier, an attacking

ll back, to mark the aggressive Jordan by sending on Wildschut to replace
ne injured Rijsbergen for the whole of the second half. The tall youngster
ook Jordan while Suurbier filled in for Rijsbergen, but Scotland went 2–1 up
hile the Dutch were still sorting themselves out. Krol was adjudged to have
uled Souness as the midfield man burst into Holland's goalmouth and Gemmill
eat Jongbloed from the penalty spot with an ease that made the memory of
Masson's miss against Peru all the more difficult to bear. The stage was now
t for the brilliant solo goal by Gemmill and four minutes of heart-in-mouth
nsion for every Scottish supporter in the stadium and around the world seeing

on television. Rep's dramatic goal dashed those short-lived hopes.

his time, MacLeod was more like his old self. 'Today,' he said defiantly, 'I
ink Scotland, the players and myself, decided to say
o hell with everyone" and go out and play.' Then in
reference to the proliferating stories about misbehaviour
the Scottish camp, he added: 'We have had a lot of
utside pressures on us – nothing to do with the game.
ontrary to what everyone thinks, it is a very
sciplined squad.' Finally, asked for a straight
nswer to the growing speculation over his future,
MacLeod replied: 'If I was thinking of resigning tonight,
if I was getting the sack tonight, I'd tell you. We'll have
to wait and see.'

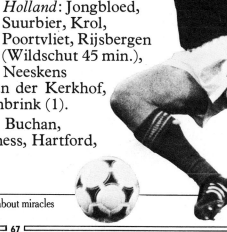

Holland: Jongbloed,
Suurbier, Krol,
Poortvliet, Rijsbergen
(Wildschut 45 min.),
Neeskens

	P	W	D	L	F	A	Pt
J	3	2	1	0	7	2	5
LAND	3	1	1	1	5	3	3
TLAND	3	1	1	1	5	6	3
J	3	0	1	2	2	8	1

oskamp 10 min.), Jansen, W. Van der Kerkhof,
. Van der Kerkhof, Rep (1), Rensenbrink (1).

otland: Rough, Kennedy, Forsyth, Buchan,
onachie, Rioch, Gemmill (2), Souness, Hartford,
rdan, Dalglish (1).

eferee: Erich Linemayr (Austria).

■ OPPOSITE. Three against three ■ Jongbloed thinks about miracles
■ Dalglish in true form at last.

Holland V Scotland

■ Rensenbrink scores the 1000th goal of the World Cup, a soft penalty — Rensenbrink's third penalty of four in Argentina.

Holland V Scotland

■ A goal worthy of the record books, Dalglish volleys past Jongbloed, and thanks Jordan for the knockdown.

CATASTROPHE IN CORDOBA

'Well,' said one Scotsman, fighting to control his bile and hysterical laughter in a Buenos Aires bar, 'I can always tell my grandchildren that I was actually present at one of *the* great Scottish disasters. Flodden Field, Culloden . . . yes, Argentina '78 was in that class.' The bitter self-mockery was revealing. It said a lot about the Scottish character and its love affair with the game of football. There has always been a streak of masochism in the Scots. They seem actually to enjoy suffering and feeling guilty. Perhaps that is why they push the self-destruct button so often. One of the more intriguing Scottish theories in the post-mortem on another of Scotland's World Cup failures was that it was all the fault of John Knox and the guilt complex driven into the national consciousness by the Calvinists and their doctrine of Predestination.

> "The trouble, in the context of a tournament as demanding and elaborate as the World Cup, is that the Scots tend to tackle their football challenges with the blind courage they invariably show on the battlefield. Planning is kept to a minimum, and almost total reliance is placed on inspiration derived from something indefinable—perhaps best described as being akin to the 'skirl of the pipes'."

An exaggerated response to disappointment in a fairly trivial sphere of human activity? For some nations, perhaps, but not for the Scots. In the absence of war and independence, football has become the expression of their national identity. The Scottish Nationalists can talk until they are blue in the face about devolution and North Sea oil: in the end, it is fitba' which unites or disunites them. The trouble, in the context of a tournament as demanding and elaborate as the World Cup, is that the Scots tend to tackle their football challenges with the blind courage they invariably show on the battlefield. Planning is kept to a minimum, and almost total reliance is placed on inspiration derived from something indefinable – perhaps best described as the 'skirl of the pipes'.

That was certainly the case in Argentina. The Scottish Football Association chose, in Ally MacLeod, a manager in the image and likeness of the Scottish public, aggressively optimistic and chauvinistic to a degree, and gambled all on the charge. They had no other choice. Willie Ormond, a man who had actually experienced the unique pressures of a World Cup, had said he did not want the Scotland manager's job any more, and Jock Stein, the most knowledgeable and respected manager in the country, kept refusing it. What that says about the SFA, I leave you to judge; nevertheless, it is true that there were few acceptable alternatives to MacLeod when Ormond withdrew. This is no attempt to absolve the SFA and MacLeod from responsibility for what happened in Argentina; but all that I have mentioned already – the Scottish penchant for self-destruction, the nation's emotional dependence on football and the deliberate choice of MacLeod for qualities which were to be his downfall – should be borne in mind when it comes to apportioning the blame.

Scotland's visit to the 1978 World Cup finals was not without distinction, of course. After all, they were the only team to beat Holland, the eventual runners-

---

■ OPPOSITE. Willie Johnston: thinking of his past as one of Scotland's most exciting wingers or of his future as the Scots player banned for life for using drugs?

up, and the only team to have one of its players dope-tested positively. It was difficult to tell which was worse. The victory over the Dutch not only served to remind us of what had been wasted in the two previous games, but encouraged the dangerous view that there was nothing really wrong with Scottish football. 'Bring on the English,' the kilted clansmen on the terraces in Cordoba were yelling irrelevantly when Scotland looked like putting enough goals past Holland to reach the last eight. Suddenly, God was in his tartan heaven again, and the only thing in the world that mattered was proving Scotland were better than England. To guilt complex, add inferiority complex.

The Willie Johnston scandal had wide repercussions, lifting the lid, as it did, on the growing use in British football of pills of one kind or another. One could pursue that issue at some length; but, for the moment, let us consider the Johnston affair as just one of many incidents which added up to a Scottish object lesson in how *not* to prepare for and approach a World Cup. MacLeod and the Scottish team doctor have sworn they made every effort to find out if any of the players was taking anything on the FIFA banned list. So their failure to discover Johnston's little habit must be put down to either sheer stupidity on the player's part or a lack of trust and communication between players and manager. It seems inconceivable that Johnston's use of stimulants did not come to light while the Scottish squad were living together at Dunblane for a week during the British Championship. Secrets do not often survive in such circumstances.

It was there, on the other side of Bannockburn from Glasgow, that the rot set in. One serious case of misbehaviour by a Scottish player is said to have been hushed up, and I know for a fact that the squad had coined a special name for the hotel basement where MacLeod used to give them their 'Up Scots, and at 'em' team talks. They called it 'the screaming room'. The name was used condescendingly by players who, for the most part, were used to more lucid and detailed briefings at their own clubs. Since then, of course, Manchester United's Lou Macari has complained bitterly about being fed a steady diet of 'We ar'ra peepel'.

There were those who suspected MacLeod of being quite mad; but his often outrageous behaviour seems to me to have been nothing more serious than an excess of nervous energy or the protective outer shell of a basically insecure person. He has the lean figure and thin, pointed features of the man who burns weight off his frame simply by keeping on the move. Mind and body are never still, and

Catastrophe in Cordoba

the variety of mental and physical contortions he managed during one of his Dunblane Press conferences was quite wonderful to behold. One Scottish sports writer said, quite rightly, that you could have sold tickets for the conferences; and another joked that, after 10 of Ally's conferences, he was on the Valium. That was the flavour of the man, restless, abrasive, outrageous; and the

media, hungry for copy, loved the taste. At that point, no-one gave a damn whether MacLeod had the tactical knowledge, experience and foresight to handle a team in the finals of the World Cup 6000 miles, and another world, away from Scotland.

Clearly, he had not. No sooner had the party arrived to a tumultuous welcome in Alta Gracia, 30 miles outside Cordoba, than the players were arguing with MacLeod and the SFA about bonuses – a subject that ought to have been sorted out long before the party left Britain – and complaining about the quality of their hotel, a relic from Britain's colonial past chosen in advance by MacLeod. The rooms, moaned the players, were too spartan, the wardrobes smelled, taps dripped, there was no games room and the television facilities were minimal. In short, they were uncomfortable and there was nothing to do. Boredom soon

■ ABOVE. MacLeod trying to find answers and putting questions to Ron Greenwood ■ OPPOSITE. The faces say it all: Peru 3-Scotland 1 ■ Ernie Walker, Secretary of the SFA, announces the decision to ban Johnston for life ■ Scotland training: no enough on a dangerous surface? ■ Macari: banned for writing for the newspapers.

Catastrophe in Cordoba

set in, and one has to be utterly naive to imagine that some drink was not taken to alleviate it. Equally, the stories of wild parties and of the Mexicans and Tunisians objecting to the late night revelry, while sharing the Sierras Hotel with the Scots, must be regarded with some circumspection. All that can be said is that the Argentinian newspapers did have a tendency to exaggerate

"The players hated the training pitch because it was easy to turn an ankle in its ruts, and those who watched the training sessions were astonished at the lack of organization and technical guidance on offer."

and the Scottish delegation did not consist entirely of players. In any case, revelry in a World Cup camp does not necessarily mean poor results on the field. The Dutch have proved that in the past.

It is necessary to understand that a major sporting event like the World Cup finals is given blanket coverage by the world's Press. Newspapers do not send just sports writers; they despatch news reporters as well to cover any stories that arise out of the sport as opposed to taking place within it. The invasion of the Israeli quarters by the Black September terrorists in Munich at the 1972 Olympic Games was the classic case. Happily, nothing so tragic happened in Argentina. The nearest the news men got to a really good story was the Willie

Catastrophe in Cordoba

Johnston business and Don Masson's fake drugs confession. In fact it was a very poor World Cup for news stories. But the news reporters still had to justify their trip to Argentina. I suspect, therefore, that not all the facts in reports picked up from the local newspapers were checked as thoroughly as might have been desirable, and that the truth was stretched here and there in the cause of keeping news editors happy back home. In fairness to my colleagues on the news side of the business, very little was in their favour. The four-hour time difference between Britain and Argentina meant that stories had to be filed early and in a rush. In addition, the distance of Scotland's hotel from Cordoba, where the British Press were obliged to live, and Argentina's unreliable internal telephone service made it extremely difficult to check facts thoroughly in the short time available. Such was the tightness of the security, too, the World Cup camps could be visited only at certain allotted times of day. Whatever the reason, the Scottish were decidedly unhappy about the bad Press they were getting in Britain. As one player said: 'If I know I deserve criticism for the way I have played, I don't mind reading it. What I do object to is being made out to be a boozer and a womanizer in a paper my wife reads.'

Physical reprisals were threatened in some cases, and MacLeod even went so far at the end of it all to blame the news reporters, and the outside pressures they exerted, for Scotland's failure on the field. It certainly made a change from blaming the players and himself by turns, but it hardly made sense. Quite clearly, MacLeod was totally unprepared for the sort of media attention that was focused on Scotland in Argentina. 'There is tremendous pressure here in Argentina,' he said after the draw with Iran. 'Whatever we do seems to make headlines. If you stop to speak to someone in the street, it gets in the papers that you were trying to get off with them.' Matters were not improved by the unco-operative attitude Scotland adopted towards the Argentinian Press from the start. Indeed, it was one of the great ironies of the situation that, for the first time, the Scots had a Press Officer in their midst.

> "If I know I deserve criticism for the way I have played, I don't mind reading it. What I do object to is being made out to be a boozer and a womanizer in a paper my wife reads," —Scottish player.

Oddly enough, Argentina's only English-language newspaper, the *Buenos Aires Herald*, was the most consistently critical. The *Herald* picked up and used stories an Argentinian agency was putting out about parties at the Sierras Hotel 'until 3 a.m.', etc. But, despite everything, other local papers bent over backwards to be fair to them. *Clarin*, for instance, restricted itself to innuendo in these reports on May 31 and June 1: 'There are all sorts of rumours about the Scots. Some are true, some are invented. Cigarettes at any time and night visits to the casino (adjoining the hotel) are real. The litres of beer and whisky and going out to "unknown" destinations – not so much' and 'It is very well known the freedom this delegation has. Their likes are divided between golf, sightseeing and drinks. And precisely the last detail gives us an anecdote. Of the 38 boxes of whisky they brought in their luggage, hardly one is left in a full, preserved state.' They also reported the Johnston scandal straight, without any of the snide references to Sir Alf Ramsey's 'animals' remark that might have been expected.

The one thing that did seem to surprise all the papers in Argentina was what they saw as the lightness and infrequency of Scotland's training. Nor were they alone in seeing inadequacies in that quarter. The players hated the training

Catastrophe in Cordoba

Córdoba

ROGAS: TODO UN ESCANDAL

Llueven críticas sobre Escocia

Johnston: tomé dos píldoras

Denuncia penal contra Johnston

Levantan restric a libertad de pre

La culpa de Johnston

Johnston reconoció el dóping

pitch because it was easy to turn an ankle in its ruts, and those who watched the training sessions were astonished at the lack of organization and technical guidance on offer. It was, I am told, training by exhortation and little else. Similarly, it has come out, in the distasteful stampede by some members of the Scottish squad to reveal all, that MacLeod was not good at giving tactical advice in the dressing room during a match. But it is pointless to rail at MacLeod for that: he was not taken on for his tactical expertise, but for his personality. What he needed was an exceptionally good coach and more support from the players.

Frankly, the attitude of some of the players was very disappointing. MacLeod's irrational team selection and rampant favouritism hardly inspired confidence, but it was reasonable to expect that professional pride alone would have ensured recognizable performances from some of the most talented players in Britain. The rigours of a long, hard season at home could not be offered, or accepted, as an excuse. As Graeme Souness said after the draw with Iran: 'These are the World Cup finals. Just being here should fill you with new life.' Martin Buchan, for one, thought the players should have shouldered the blame. The Manchester United captain, a mature personality with an independent streak, made the point that it was the players and not the manager who went out on the field to kick the ball. It disturbed Buchan, too, to discover that some of the squad did not realize how much they had let themselves and the Scottish supporters down.

Buchan's point is a good one. If Scotland had scored just one more goal against Iran, everything – the doubts about MacLeod's technical ability as a manager, the misgivings about his commercial exploitation of the World Cup to the tune of an estimated £50,000 and the implications of the Willie Johnston drug scandal – would have been forgotten in the joy of reaching the second round. As it was, Scotland badly underestimated Peru and Iran and started playing, against Holland, only when their backs were to the wall in the Group. Exactly whose fault that was, we shall probably never know. MacLeod should have gone to watch Scotland's opponents beforehand; but, equally, the players had enough experience between them to work things out for themselves when the football did not go according to plan. ('What plan?' said one player sarcastically.) Perhaps, as I suggested at the beginning, the Scottish national character was the real culprit.

■ The Argentinian Spanish Press treatment of Johnston.

GROUP A

If West Germany played with an eye on tactical points in Group Two, their efforts gained them little advantage in the second round. Group A was composed, as agreed beforehand, of the winners of Groups One and Three and the runners-up of Groups Two and Four. Since none of the four first rounds groups panned out exactly as had been expected, the West Germans found themselves bracketed with three strong European sides, one of which, Italy, had the look of potential world champions. Having beaten France, Hungary and Argentina convincingly, the Italians were now clear favourites to represent this group in the final. Confidence and job satisfaction were coming out of the players' ears, and their teamwork was second to none. Only Antognoni, who was having severe domestic problems, had failed to shine, but the industrious Zaccarelli was gaining in stature every time he was substituted for the graceful touch player from Fiorentina.

Like West Germany, Holland had looked decidedly out of sorts in the first round. The Dutch had less excuse because they had lost far fewer players from 1974 than the West Germans. In fact, they had lost only one – Johan Cruyff – and his loss to Holland was certainly no greater than that of Franz Beckenbauer to West Germany. What, then, had gone wrong with the Dutch out in the Andes? From the beginning, the players had been complaining about the effects of altitude. Nosebleeds were common at the Dutch training headquarters, 6000 ft above sea level, and the players reckoned that the tiring effect of altitude, combined with the long grass on the pitch at the spectacularly-sited Mendoza stadium, had, between them, prevented Holland from playing their normal, high-pressure football.

"The Dutch had less excuse because they had lost far fewer players from 1974 than the West Germans. In fact, they had lost only one—Johan Cruyff—and his loss to Holland was certainly no greater than that of Franz Beckenbauer to West Germany."

There were other man-made problems. The Dutch players had been bewildered by Ernst Happel's tactical switches from one game to the next. In the first three matches, he had employed three different formations, 3-4-3, 3-5-2 and 4-4-2, and the team was clearly unhappy about the lack of managerial consistency and a settled style of play. Rifts were also evident within the playing ranks. In the tense, anxious, unhappy atmosphere of Mendoza, the Van der Kerkhof twins, Willy and Rene, who play for PSV Eindhoven, complained that their captain, Ruud Krol, an Ajax man, had no right to criticize them on the field since he was making more mistakes than anyone himself. Thus, the old inter-club jealousies, the bane of Dutch soccer, had resurfaced.

The wider criticism of Happel included, too, the complaints that he was not allowing Rensenbrink the free role in which he does so much damage for Anderlecht and that he was relying too heavily on the 'old guard' from 1974 at the expense of promising youngsters like Poortvliet, Wildschut and Brandts. Poortvliet, strong, mobile and versatile in the classic Dutch manner, had played against Peru and Scotland; but Wildschut, it was argued, would not have got on against the Scots if Rijsbergen had not been injured. And Brandts? Ah, yes.

■ Young Mr Brandts delights Rep, Rene Van der Kerkof and Rensenbrink. Cabrini, Scirea, Benetti, Gentile, Cucureddu, Zaccarelli and Bettega are suitably surprised ■ The Dutch twins, Willy and Rene Van der Kerkof.

We were to know a lot more about young Mr Brandts before Group A had finished.

The Austrians had certainly been more successful than the Dutch at disguising their internal conflicts. Few, seeing them march over Spain and Sweden, would have credited the stories about animosity between the team manager, Helmut Senekowitsch, and the general manager, Max Merkel, and of ill-feeling among the players over a 'perks' pool that had been confined to the Austrians not playing abroad. They had established themselves as a well-organized team with a strong defence, but their heavy reliance upon Krankl for goals seemed to limit their prospects of further advancement in a group that guaranteed Europe one finalist.

W.GERMANY V ITALY

The second Wednesday of the 1978 World Cup dawned in fog, and the mist had not cleared properly as the crowd for this eagerly-anticipated confrontation began to assemble at the River Plate Stadium about lunchtime. Inside, however, the visibility was good enough to allay any fears of a postponement. So we settled ourselves down to re-examine the popular theories about the two teams and to hope romantically for a game as entertaining as the high-scoring cliffhanger between them in the quarter finals of the 1970 World Cup. In that direction, I am afraid, lay only disappointment. West Germany returned to Buenos Aires with all the caution they had shown in the inaugural match, and it soon became obvious that they put not losing above winning in their order of priorities on this occasion.

The first clue to their intentions was the selection of Zimmermann and Holzenbein in preference to the two Müllers, Dieter and Hansi. 'To beat Italy,' Ron Greenwood, the England manager, said before the match, 'you have got to find a way of isolating Benetti.' And Zimmermann was clearly brought into the midfield with that sort of operation in mind. Holzenbein and Rummenigge, the nominal wingers, joined him, Bonhof and Flohe there frequently, too, as the West Germans fell back in strength at any hint of danger from the Italians. The following day, Dino Zoff, Italy's goalkeeper and captain, was to say: 'For years we were derided as the team that could survive only by using _catenaccio_ defence (man-to-man marking with a sweeper). So you can imagine our feelings when West Germany, the world champions, were forced to use _catenaccio_ to keep us out. Now we have become known as an attacking team.'

Unfortunately, reputations cannot be cashed in for goals, and Italy were left to rue one uncharacteristic and costly aberration by Bettega in front of goal and two goalline clearances by the West Germans. Perhaps we should have sensed that Italy would never score when Scirea (the Italians' sweeper, no less!) joined the attack brilliantly down the left three minutes before half time. His perfect centre was missed by Vogts, Bettega's shadow, and chested down in textbook fashion by the tall, elegant Italian striker. Then, to the horror of the large Italian following (Buenos Aires has a populous Italian quarter – Boca), Bettega, normally so cool and clinical in the penalty area, prodded the ball wide from little more than six yards.

By then, West Germany had already cleared off the line once. Kaltz saved the day with his trailing heel when a gorgeous pass from Causio sent Bettega swerving past Maier for an angled shot at the yawning goal. Bettega was the sufferer in the second half, too, when the ball was again stopped on the West German line by a defender. The Italian had let fly after a cunning chip by Cabrini, the left back, had hit the inside of the far post and come out. Italy's last real chance materialized when Zaccarelli, who had replaced Antognoni at half time, got behind the West German defence to meet Tardelli's long centre at the far post. Zaccarelli's downward header was firm and true, but Maier's dive enabled him to push the ball clear.

Maier, in fact, broke the World Cup record in this game for not conceding a goal. It had been held from 1966 by England's Gordon Banks, who kept a clean sheet for 438 minutes – or nearly four matches. Maier's was not a record to be particularly proud of, however, because West Germany had done little else but ry to stop their opponents scoring. Three goalless draws were a more accurate reflection of their form and attitude than the 6–0 victory over the demoralized Mexicans. Still, one could not help but again admire the West Germans' efficiency as they made the best of their limited resources. They were down to nine players at one point in the second half, while Flohe and Fischer both received treatment behind the Italian goal for injuries. Fischer returned, but Beer came on for Flohe, whose leg injury put him out of action for the rest of the tournament.

It was a sad ending to perhaps Flohe's best game. Twice he had gotten into scoring positions without reward, and once he created a shot for Rummenigge that was deflected narrowly wide by Cabrini. But the best of the West Germans' infrequent scoring attempts had been a snap volley by Holzenbein after 25 minutes. Zoff cannot have seen the ball until late, but he stopped it with the sort of sure, flying save that he was unable to repeat in subsequent matches. So, the Italian march on the final had been halted, and West Germany were still in with a chance themselves.

West Germany: Maier, Vogts, Rüssmann, Kaltz, Dietz, Bonhof, Flohe (Beer 58 min.), Zimmermann (Konopka 53 min.), Rummenigge, Fischer, Holzenbein.
Italy: Zoff, Gentile, Bellugi, Scirea, Cabrini, Tardelli, Benetti, Antognoni (Zaccarelli 45 min.), Causio, Rossi, Bettega.
Referee: Dusan Maksimovic (Yugoslavia).

■ The last of Zoff's great saves? ■ They cannot believe Bettega has missed.

AUSTRIA V HOLLAND

Holland's complaints about the handicaps of playing at Mendoza were given credibility by their comprehensive destruction of Austria at Cordoba. Away from the altitude and long grass of the Andean city, the Dutch suddenly burst into goal-scoring life. In another respect, this gargantuan victory was a happy accident. For the injuries sustained against Scotland by Neeskens, Suurbier and Rijsbergen obliged Ernst Happel to rely on the youngsters his critics had been urging him to bring in. Happel had already expressed his faith in Poortvliet, but now he was forced to retain Wildschut, a second half substitute against Scotland, and to blood the untried Erny Brandts, 22. Neeskens' absence also necessitated the recall of Haan in midfield, and Happel's dissatisfaction with Jongbloed's goalkeeping gave the roly-poly Schrijvers his first taste of action in this World Cup.

Despite the scoreline, Schrijvers was often busy in the first half. After Brandts had celebrated his introduction by heading fiercely past Koncilia in the sixth minute, the Dutch goalkeeper had to save with his feet from Jara. He was also indebted to Brandts for saving the situation when Jara, dangerous on the left, drew him from his goal and passed to Krankl. Indeed, Austria seemed about to equalize when Holland suddenly knocked them sideways with two goals in as many minutes. Rensenbrink scored the first after 35 minutes by stroking home his fourth penalty and fifth goal of the tournament, and Rep got the second of the brace when, with the Austrian defence failing to cut out a centre from Rensenbrink, he lobbed the ball over the advancing Koncilia.

The match had begun in mist and drizzle, and the slippery pitch was responsible for many of the match's defensive errors. The Austrian defence, always ready to concede free kicks, seemed more ill at ease in the conditions and it was no surprise when Rep (53 minutes) and Willy Van der Kerkhof (72 minutes) increased Holland's lead in the second half to an extent that made Obermayer's consolation goal for Austria (70 minutes) little more than a defiant gesture. Though not all observers were convinced that Holland had struck World Cup-winning form, there could be no doubt that this establishment of a healthy goal difference had put the Dutch firmly in the driving seat of Group A from the start.

Austria: Koncilia, Sara, Pezzey, Obermayer (1), Breitenberger, Prohaska, Hickersberger, Kreiger, Jara, Kreuz, Krankl.

Holland: Schrijvers, Brandts (1) (Van Kraaij 66 min.), Krol, Wildschut, Poortvliet, Jansen, Haan, W. Van Der Kerkhof (1), Rep (2), Rensenbrink (1), R. Van der Kerkhof.

Referee: John Gordon (Scotland).

OPPOSITE. Schrijvers dives but Brandts saves ■ ABOVE. John Gordon watches Sara and Krol exchange pennants ■ The twins congratulate Johnny Rep ■ Obermayer slips as Wildschut dives in ■ Schrijvers takes a quick goalkick.

HOLLAND V W.GERMANY

Holland could hardly wait for this gunfight in Argentinian cowboy territory. For four years, the Dutch had tortured themselves with the thought that they had thrown the game away when West Germany beat them 2–1 in the final of the 1974 World Cup, and now they wanted revenge. Determination oozed out of every pore as the kick-off approached. 'It's not a vendetta,' said Ernst Happel, 'but the players do want to set the record straight.' They had to be fancied to do it, too. While Holland were blitzing Austria 5–1, the West Germans had offered no sign of a similar improvement while frustrating Italy in their goalless draw. The Dutch were the team in form, and it seemed most unlikely that the fading West Germans could raise their game sufficiently to hold Holland.

Even at their weakest, however, West Germany can never be written off. Knowing they dared not lose if any hope of reaching the final was to remain, they forced the pace at once and took the lead after only three minutes. Abramczik, recalled to the attack together with Dieter Müller, scored the goal by diving forward to head past Schrijvers when Bonhof at last made a free kick tell and the Dutch goalkeeper could not hold his thunderbolt. Holland's mood at that point could be judged by the tackle on the lively Abramczik that earned Willy Van der Kerkhof a booking a few minutes after the winger's goal. Once the red mist had cleared, though, Holland began to play some constructive, purposeful football. Rensenbrink, more recognizable now as the deadly will-o'-the-wisp of European club conflicts, went close with a free kick and a header before Haan brought the crowd of 46,000 to their feet with one of the most spectacular goals of the 1978 World Cup. Allowed to move forward unchallenged from midfield, as Rep had been by Scotland on the same pitch, Haan looked up from 25 yards out and smashed a rising shot into the top, right-hand corner of Maier's net. So expertly placed was the ball, and so great its velocity, that the goalkeeper did not even attempt to stop the first goal he had conceded in the tournament. Rep was only inches away from scoring a second Dutch goal immediately afterwards, but West German discipline and resilience gave them the rest of the first half, Schrijvers having to save from Bonhof, Beer and Abramczik. They stayed on top for the first 25 minutes of the second half, too, and Dieter Müller looked to have struck a decisive blow when he headed in a fine Beer centre to make it 2–1 after 70 minutes. 'God is with us,' said a watching West German half jokingly, half thankfully as Rep flew past three defenders and slapped the crossbar with his shot. Few were prepared to argue, either, while Abramczik was proving troublesome again and Schrijvers was having to make a splendid reflex save to keep out a thunderous Beer volley. Holland, it seemed, were destined to lose again to their old foes.

With 12 minutes left to play, the Dutch made a last, desperate throw by sending on the tall, upright Nanninga for Wildschut and pushing forward in strength. Nanninga, an orthodox centre forward, is the antithesis of the classic Dutch all-purpose player, and whenever he was brought on as substitute Holland were virtually admitting their impotence without Johan Cruyff; but, this time, Nanninga helped to create the right, aggressive climate for Rene Van der Kerkhof to cut in from the left like a dagger, draw Maier off his line and shoot past him. Rüssmann dived to try to stop the ball with his hands, but it was to no avail. Holland had equalized for the second time seven minutes from the end and reduced Group A to virtually a two-horse race between themselves and Italy.

Nor was that the end of the drama. In the last minute Nanninga was sent off in farcical circumstances. He and Holzenbein were indulging in some in-

fighting while waiting for a corner to be taken, and Nanninga replied with an elbow in the ribs when Holzenbein took hold of the Dutch striker by the nose. Complete chaos followed. In a milling throng, the referee did not seem sure who had done what, and he looked as surprised as everyone else when Rene Van der Kerkhof walked off the pitch. The Dutch winger had only gone to tell an amused Dutch bench what had happened, however, and Nanninga, too, could see the funny side of the incident when he was eventually ordered off.

Holland: Schrijvers, Brandts, Krol, Wildschut (Nanninga 78 min.), Poortvliet, Jansen, Haan (1), W. Van der Kerkhof, Rep, Rensenbrink, R. Van der Kerkhof (1).

West Germany: Maier, Vogts, Rüssmann, Kaltz, Dietz, Bonhof, Beer, Rummenigge, Abramczik (1), D. Müller (1), Holzenbein.

Referee: Ramon Barreto Ruiz (Uruguay).

OPPOSITE. Sepp Maier has a tight grip on the ball . . . ■ ABOVE. . . . but he could not get a hand to Rene Van der Kerkof's shot after the Dutchman had evaded this flying tackle from Manfred Kaltz.

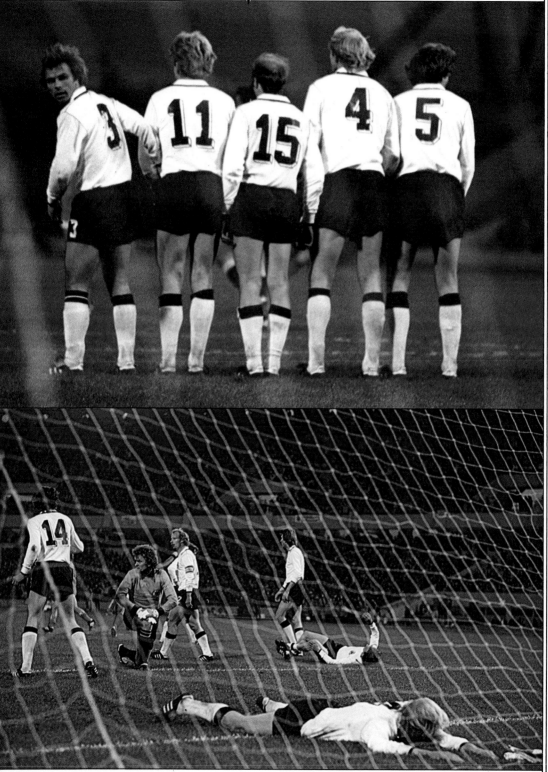

OPPOSITE. Bonhof is faced by a seven-man wall but he gets round it and Schrijvers can only push the ball out to Abramczik ho heads home ■ Ramon Barreto explains the situation and Nanninga's appeal is futile ■ ABOVE. 'Are you ready, Sepp', says Dietz ■ But later Rüssman is unable to stop Rene Van der Kerkof's equalizer.

ITALY V AUSTRIA

An air of pessimism and self-doubt suddenly enveloped the Italian camp between their failure to beat West Germany and this match. After the goalless draw with the West Germans, Italy's first setback of the tournament, Enzo Bearzot had said his team had come to Argentina not to win the World Cup but to demonstrate the progress Italian football had made. 'We were delighted to make the second round, so anything else is a bonus,' he added, somewhat defensively. Bearzot took up the same theme the following morning, saying: 'My work on the Italian team began three years ago and it is not finished yet. This World Cup is just one of the legs on the journey towards the teamwork and versatility I have been trying to achieve.'

One look at the Italian manager told how much the strain of the competition was telling on him. Drawn and tense, he wore the hunted look of a stag at bay as, hemmed in by Italian media men at the Hindu Country Club, Italy's headquarters 30 miles outside Buenos Aires, he reminded the world that Italy had had a harder programme than any of the other finalists. Against his better judgment, he had yielded to the pleas of his happy, confident team not to field several reserves, and conserve energy, against Argentina in the final game of Group One; and now, clearly, he could sense the mental and physical fatigue of his players.

The dullness of Italy's victory over Austria was therefore predictable. Lacking their normal sparkle, the Italians fell back on defence, as they used to do in the bad old days, once they had taken the lead through Rossi after 13 minutes. Significantly, their best performances were in defence, where Gentile marked Kreuz out of the game and Scirea added to his reputation for solidity. Tardelli was lively enough in midfield, too, but the lack of support given him by others caused whistles of derision from the half-filled stadium and many of the crowd left early to be sure of catching Argentina's crucial Group B match against Poland on television that night.

Austria were even less enterprising than Italy. Prohaska, their chief creative force, was often to be seen in defence and the two changes they made following their drubbing by Holland, Strasser for Breitenberger at left back and Schachner, a striker, for Kreiger, a midfield man, effected no improvement. In fact, it was Strasser who made the mistake that gave Rossi his goal. Under pressure from Causio and Rossi, Strasser unwisely chose to pass back to Koncilia instead of conceding a corner and Rossi nipped in to score. Austria's confidence, badly shaken by Holland, collapsed completely at that point. Krankl spent the game as a lone raider and only Koncilia, who resisted all of Italy's spasmodic second half attacks, emerged with any real credit.

Italy: Zoff, Gentile, Bellugi (Cuccureddu 45 min.), Scirea, Cabrini, Tardelli, Benetti, Zaccarelli, Causio, Rossi (1), Bettega (Graziani 71 min.).

Austria: Koncilia, Sara, Pezzey, Obermayer, Strasser, Prohaska, Hickersberger, Jara, Kreuz, Krankl, Schachner (Pirkner 63 min.).

Referee: Francis Rion (Belgium).

■ Jubilant Paolo Rossi leaves Koncilia helpless and Sara dismayed after Strasser had passed back weakly.

AUSTRIA V W.GERMANY

Austria's contribution to the 1978 World Cup ended on a high note, that of West Germany on a low one. While the Austrians went home consoled by their first victory over West Germany for 47 years, their European neighbours inflicted a sad ending on the dazzling 14-year career of Helmut Schön as their manager. The 62-year old who had steered West Germany to one World Cup win, one second place and one third place in the previous three tournaments deserved a worthier farewell than this defeat as he prepared to hand over the reins to his successor, Jupp Derwall. In the end, though, this moderately good West German team simply did not have the capacity to put on a show for their departing chief.

Having taken the lead through Rummenigge after 19 minutes and having held it until the 60th minute, when Vogts conceded an own goal, West Germany were destroyed by two superb second half goals from the irrepressible Krankl, whose second shot nullified Holzenbein's equalizer. Austria, well led by Sara, won the game in midfield where West Germany offered little resistance to their opponents' industry, aggression and creativeness. Prohaska, well supported by Kreuz, was outstanding in that vital area of the field, and the West German defence proved vulnerable to the pace and finishing that had made Krankl a prime target for the richer Spanish and West German clubs.

Vogts, the West German captain and another familiar figure due to retire from the international scene after these finals, brought the game to life on the hour by deflecting a Schachner header past Maier. Krankl volleyed his first goal with his left foot after 66 minutes, but Austria allowed Holzenbein to head another equalizer from Bonhof's free kick a minute later. The introduction of Hansi Müller and Fischer gave West Germany the upper hand for a time, yet both sides seemed to have settled for a draw when Krankl suddenly picked up the ball wide on the left three minutes from time. Brushing past the towering Rüssmann and cutting inside little Vogts, Krankl steered the ball wide of Maier to give Austria a satisfying, if meaningless, victory and leave Argentina with a spectacular reminder of his prowess as a striker.

Austria: Koncilia, Sara, Pezzey, Obermayer, Strasser, Prohaska, Hickersberger, Sara, Schachner (Oberacher 71 min.), Krankl (2), Kreuz.

West Germany: Maier, Vogts (o.g.), Rüssmann, Kaltz, Dietz, Bonhof, Beer (H. Müller 45 min.), Holzenbein (1), Abramczik, D. Müller (Fischer 60 min.), Rummenigge (1).

Referee: Abraham Klein (Israel).

■ Vogts the West German captain due to retire from the international scene after these finals brought the game to life.

HOLLAND V ITALY

HOLLAND V ITALY

Holland qualified for the final of the World Cup for the second successive time when nothing seemed less likely. Outplayed in the first half and fortunate to be only one goal behind at half time, they drew on their reserves of character to steamroll Italy to defeat after the interval with hard, sometimes brutal, tackling and two more high-velocity shots which were becoming such a feature of this World Cup. Angel Martinez, the Spanish referee, was not firm enough by any standards, and Enzo Bearzot, Italy's manager, was to leave Argentina still complaining bitterly about the Dutch tactics in the second half.

Italy had only themselves to blame for their defeat, however. They wasted too many chances in the first half for comfort and they allowed themselves to be provoked into indiscretion, and to be unsettled generally, by Holland's aggression. It is tempting, too, to castigate the Italians for not making their half time lead stick. Being 1–0 up with half the game gone used to be a perfect recipe for victory to the ultra-defensive Italian sides of the past. But to criticize Italy on that score is to write off all the progressive, painstaking work done by Bearzot to bring Italian football out of its Dark Age, and make a constructive contribution to the world game.

In this win-or-bust situation Italy went on the attack immediately in the manner we had come to expect. Before the game was ten minutes old, Rossi had skimmed the bar with a header and Cabrini had frittered away a glorious scoring chance. Put clear by Causio's marvellous through pass, the attacking full back shot wildly over the bar with Rossi and Bettega pleading in front of goal for a pass. Schrijvers had to come off his line quickly, too, to snatch the ball away from Rossi and Causio as the Dutch defence was cut to pieces by Italy's quick, accurate and incisive attacks. The Italians were almost too eager at times. Causio, for instance, was caught offside at the far post at the climax of a velvety move between Zaccarelli, preferred from the start to Antognoni and playing supremely well, Bettega and Benetti.

Nothing was more inevitable than the Italian goal after 19 minutes. A rapid interchange of passes outside the Dutch penalty area did not quite come off, but a favourable break of the ball sent Bettega striding clear. He hesitated as he approached Schrijvers and the ball became entangled in his feet. At that

moment, however, Brandts chose to make a desperate sliding tackle from behind that not only steered the ball into the net but cut the knee of Schrijvers badly as he threw himself at Bettega's feet. The injury was serious enough for the goalkeeper to be carried off on a stretcher, and Holland had to wait for a replacement, Jongbloed, before they could tackle the problem of overhauling Italy.

Jongbloed distinguished himself immediately by turning a Rossi volley round a post after a bad mistake by Krol and then saving another volley,

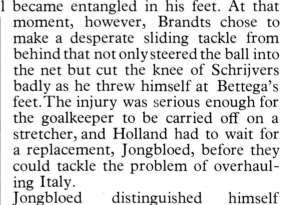

even more ferocious, from Benetti. It was then, after that impressive display of agility by a 'cold' goalkeeper, that the rough stuff started. Haan kicked the prostrate Zaccarelli because he himself had been kicked by Benetti; Rep flattened Benetti; and, finally, Benetti fouled Rensenbrink cruelly in response to the ill-treatment he had received from Rep. At least one of them should have gone off, but Senor Martinez contented himself with booking Rep belatedly and taking Benetti's name. It was Benetti's second caution of the tournament, and the Italians went in at half time knowing they would be without their hard, influential midfield player if they reached the final.

It was during the interval that all the crucial decisions were made. While Ernst Happel rectified his mistake of setting Neeskens to mark Rossi by giving the job to the better-equipped Jansen, Enzo Bearzot, obviously convinced that Italy had the game won, elected to save Causio for the final and replace him with Claudio Sala. The latter, an erroneous substitution to rank with that of Sir Alf Ramsey when he took off Bobby Charlton while England were leading West Germany in the 1970 quarter finals, proved to be the Italian manager's one serious mistake of this tournament. Italy, without Causio, lost momentum and Holland, with Neeskens pressing forward, gained it.

Three minutes into the second half, Zoff was tipping over the bar a header from Neeskens; and, two minutes later, Holland were on level terms. Atoning spectacularly for his first half own goal, young Brandts cleared up a confused situation outside the Italian penalty area by battering a first-time shot past Zoff. From then until Holland scored the winner it was total mayhem. Haan was booked for tripping Rossi; Rep was lucky not to be sent off for throwing himself at Cuccureddu as he had at Benetti; Cabrini's name was taken for a foul on Haan; Benetti elbowed Neeskens in the face; and Tardelli's name joined the long list in the referee's notebook for committing one of a sickening succession of fouls.

In that context, Haan's winning goal was a rose among thorns. Picking up a short free kick 35 yards out, the Dutch midfield player moved forward a step or two, steadied himself and then unleashed a truly venomous shot. Zoff, slow to anticipate the danger, got a hand to the ball as he threw himself to his left but could only help the shot in off the inside of the far post. Italy's substitution of Graziani for Benetti two minutes later was little more than an empty gesture, and the remaining period of the game was a procession of Dutch attacks led by Rensenbrink, who really ought to have scored with a free header in the first half.

	P	W	D	L	F	A	Pt
HOLLAND	3	2	1	0	9	4	5
ITALY	3	1	1	1	2	2	3
W GERMANY	3	0	2	1	4	5	2
AUSTRIA	3	1	0	2	4	8	2

Holland: Schrijvers (Jongbloed 21 min.), Brandts (o.g.,1), Krol, Neeskens, Poortvliet, Jansen, Haan (1), W. Van der Kerkhof, Rep, Rensenbrink, R. Van der Kerkhof.
Italy: Zoff, Cuccureddu, Gentile, Scirea, Cabrini, Tardelli, Benetti (Graziani 77 min.), Zaccarelli, Causio (C. Sala 46 min.), Rossi, Bettega.
Referee: Angel Martinez (Spain).

■ PREVIOUS PAGE. Balletic poses form a background to Bettega's jubilation as Ernie Brandts not only scores an own goal but kicks Schrijvers' face ■ OPPOSITE. The biter bit: Neeskens gets a grip on Benetti ■ The Italians reach a peak of jubilation after Brandts' own goal. They think Bettega has scored.

TOP. Cabrini hits a fierce shot but Schrijvers pushes it well over ■ ABOVE AND OPPOSITE. The Italians can't believe it but Arie Haan knows it's there: in the net from 35 yards and in the final for the second time in succession.

GROUP B

POLAND PERU ARGENTINA BRAZIL

Poland's reward for overcoming West Germany and winning Group Two was to find themselves in Group B with three South American sides – one of them the hosts, Argentina. There was, therefore, a chance that Europe would monopolize the final, though it seemed very remote. The Poles had not played well enough in the first round to justify any great hopes of their reaching the final, and the problem of facing three opponents with whom they were relatively unfamiliar seemed difficult. Added to that was the fanatical support Argentina could expect wherever they appeared. It had been assumed by Europeans that Argentina had lost an advantage by being evicted from the River Plate Stadium; but knowledgeable locals pointed out gleefully that the stadium at Rosario would be even more intimidating for Argentina's opponents than its larger counterpart in Buenos Aires. Though it held only 40,000 people, as against the River Plate's capacity of 78,000, the crowd was right on top of the pitch and the sound waves were, therefore, that much more numbing in the tightly-enclosed space.

Argentina's only problems were the possible psychological effect of having been beaten by Italy in their last match and the injury which had kept Luque out of that game. Kempes' effectiveness had been much diminished by his partner's absence, and there was little hope that Luque's dislocated elbow would mend quickly enough for him to play in Argentina's first Group B match, against Poland. A further twist had been given to the situation by the death of Luque's brother in a dreadful road accident on the eve of the game against Italy.

There was encouragement for Poland, certainly, in the first round form of Peru and Brazil. Though the Peruvians had given fair warning of their attacking

expertise, Poland looked to have a defence strong enough to withstand their shimmering advances. Sooner or later, too, someone had to take that sketchy defence of theirs to the cleaners. Brazil were the exact opposite of Peru in that they had revealed a sound defence and a toothless attack. Brazil's well-advertised internal conflicts also suggested that morale in their camp would be less than perfect in the second round.

Brazil, in fact, went into Group B under protest. As they had finished Group Three on the same number of points as Austria, four, with exactly the same goal difference, they had invoked a long-forgotten clause in the FIFA regulations which stated that, in the event of such a tie, the group winners would be decided by lot. After due consideration, however, FIFA decided to uphold the regulation which stated that the group winners would be the team which had scored the greater number of goals. Thus, Austria were nominated as the winners of Group Three and Brazil were shunted into Group B with Argentina – their oldest and most deadly South American rivals.

BRAZIL V PERU

All at once, Brazil started playing to something like their full potential. Though Zico, Reinaldo, Edinho and Rivelino were still out of favour, the existing combination discovered enough inspiration and cohesion to exploit Peru's uncertain defence. Quiroga, whose goalkeeping had often owed as much to good luck as to good judgment, ran out of both commodities completely as Brazil put him under fire from the start. Twice he was beaten by Dirceu from 30 yards in the first half hour, and Peru, for all their typically spirited attacking, never really recovered from that double blow.

They were struggling from the moment, 11 minutes after the start, that Diaz, their left back, was injured and Navarro, a reserve, had to be drafted into an already creaking defence. Quiroga saved well enough from Roberto, fed by the enterprising Dirceu, but he was powerless to stop the sensational free kick Dirceu swerved into the top corner after a quarter of an hour. That shot must have induced shell-shock because Quiroga let the ball go under his body the next time Dirceu let fly from a good distance in the 27th minute.

Leao, too, was far from idle. Peru's splendid wingers were getting behind the Brazilian defence, and the goalkeeper had to summon every ounce of his skill and agility to keep out shots from Munante and Cueto and to preserve Brazil's 2–0 lead until the interval. Then, in the second half, Leao was required to save from Cueto and the dangerous La Rosa before Zico, introduced for Gil with 20 minutes to go, pushed the match out of Peru's reach by scoring from the penalty awarded after 72 minutes for the first of two crude fouls on the battered Roberto.

Brazil: Leao, Toninho, Oscar, Amaral, Rodrigues Neto, Cerezo (Chicao 76 min.), Batista, Dirceu (2), Gil (Zico 70 min. (1)), Roberto, Mendonca.

Peru: Quiroga, Duarte, Manzo, Chumpitaz, Diaz (Navarro 11 min.), Velasquez, Cubillas, Cueto, Munante, La Rosa, Oblitas (P. Rojas 45 min.).

Referee: Nicolai Rainea (Romania).

■ OPPOSITE. Luque: injury and tragedy stopped him playing ■ Quiroga completely misses Dirceu's amazing free kick.

POLAND V ARGENTINA

JUNE 14 ROSARIO GROUP B POLAND 0 ARGENTINA 2

'Mario Alberto Kempes . . . Goool!!!' I can still hear the excited Argentinian television commentator elongating the vowel sounds of the vital word in his stratospheric, celebratory wail. The litany is burned into the memories of all those who watched Argentina's matches live or recorded, on the box in Argentina, and this was the commentator's first opportunity to recite it. Twice Kempes broke his World Cup duck, and twice his countrymen went mad with joy. It was a bravura performance by the tall, dark, athletic Argentinian, one that stamped him beyond question as a footballer of true world class. With a pinch more steadiness, Kempes would have crowned a coruscating display of all the attacking skills with a spectacular hat-trick.

Three goals against, though, would have been more than Poland deserved to concede. Disciplined, organized and experienced, the Poles made a sterling contribution to a fine contest in which Argentina had need of all Kempes' gifts to survive. Bravely resisting the razor-edged patriotic fervour of the packed Rosario crowd, Poland put Argentina under extreme pressure between Kempes' two goals – scored in the 14th and 71st minutes – and should have equalized from a first half penalty. By now, Lubanski's disappointing form had persuaded the Poles to cut their losses and settle into a 4–4–2 formation which relied on the ability of Deyna and Boniek to come from midfield to score. Nawalka, too, was blossoming nicely as an attacking midfield player at the tender age of 20. Twice in the first half, the strategy worked so well that Fillol was hard pressed to keep out a fierce rising shot and then a powerful header from the rampaging Boniek, 22, another of Poland's promising young newcomers. And Poland were in full cry again when the ubiquitous Kempes made a great one-handed save on the line after 39 minutes. Deyna, the cool, seasoned Polish captain, rarely

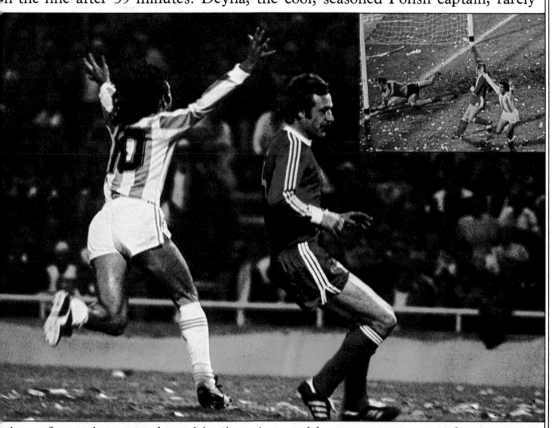

misses from the spot; but this time he could not muster enough power or accuracy of shot to beat the dive which made Fillol an instant national hero. That was virtually Poland's last chance of saving the game. Lato shot into the side-netting early in the second half, but the time was approaching when Kempes would reassert himself imperiously and decisively.

His first intervention had come when Bertoni, out on the left touchline, sent a high centre towards the near post. Racing in diagonally across the penalty area, Kempes timed his arrival to perfection. Dipping his flowing black locks fractionally in front of a Polish defender, he glided the ball past Tomaszewski with all the finesse of a latter-day Tommy Lawton. It was difficult to decide

■ At last! At last! Mario Kempes breaks his duck and shows his joy to Bertoni and the world.

Argentina V Poland

which was the better goal, that one or his second. Ardiles, a consummate midfield player who, strangely, was not rated as highly by the Argentinian people as by British television viewers, did much of the spade work by carrying the ball up to the Polish penalty area and giving Kempes a pass that put him in sight of goal. Exploding into action, the striker went on to his favourite left foot, dragged the ball clear of a Polish defender on the edge of the penalty area and drilled a low shot wide of Tomaszewski's left hand.

Kempes was full of himself now, and the Gorgon-less Polish defence melted away from him once more as he burst through in the last minute to drive the ball into the side-netting. But there was much more to Kempes' performance than sheer marksmanship. In addition to his two goals, he also offered Bertoni and Houseman opportunities to score and generally dominated Poland with the

sweep of his talent. Above all, Kempes had proved himself capable of great things without the convalescing Luque. Operating alone as Argentina's central striker, instead of breaking from slightly deeper as he had before, the great man not only established his own singularity but lifted Argentina's confidence and morale to new heights.

Poland: Tomaszewski, Szymanowski, Zmuda, Kasperczak, Maculewicz, Masztaler (Mazur 66 min.), Deyna, Boniek, Nawalka, Lato, Szarmach.

Argentina: Fillol, Olguin, L. Galvan, Passarella, Tarantini, Ardiles, Gallego, Valencia (Villa 45 min.), Houseman (Ortiz 83 min.), Kempes (2), Bertoni.

Referee: Ulf Eriksson (Sweden).

■ ABOVE. Superstitious Kempes shaved and wore a bandage ■ OPPOSITE. Quiroga, unlucky to be booked.

98

PERU V POLAND

If Poland had reached double figures out in mountain country, Peru could not have complained. With the possible exception of West Germany's slaughter of the Mexicans, there can have been no more one-sided match than this in the 1978 World Cup. It was a procession of Polish attacks interrupted only occasionally by the Peruvian forwards, and the South Americans were deeply indebted to Quiroga, a remarkable goalkeeper in more ways than one, for their escape from a thorough trouncing. Nawalka really came into his own on this occasion, and he, Deyna and Boniek presented the notoriously brittle Peruvian defence with endless problems. In contrast, the Polish defence, strengthened by the return of Gorgon, coped well with Peru's two variations on an attacking theme, one-twos through the middle and speed on the wings.

Basically, the action was a catalogue of Polish shots and headers at goal. In all, Quiroga made seven creditable saves, one of them when Deyna headed a Szarmach cross against a post and Lato headed the rebound into the Peruvian goalkeeper's arms. That was the second time Poland had hit the woodwork. In the first half, a shot from Nawalka was deflected on to the bar and over it. In addition, Deyna, twice, and Lato were within feet of scoring as Peru lost all credibility as quarterfinalists. Munante and Oblitas often circumvented the Polish defence, but without causing undue trouble. The crossing and shooting of Oblitas, in particular, was wastefully wild, and Kukla had a quiet time of it as deputy for Tomaszewski, Poland's injured goalkeeper.

For all their superiority, however, Poland had to wait a long time for their goal. But it was well worth the wait when it finally arrived after 65 minutes. A Peruvian defender, Navarro, generously gave the ball away to Lato on the right touchline, and his centre was driven into the net by the totally unmarked Szarmach with a spectacular diving header. Quiroga was beaten at last, but far from finished. Living up to his nickname of 'El Loco', he came out to the

halfway line to break up a Polish attack two minutes from the end. Then, a minute later, he advanced well into the Polish half to rugby-tackle Lato. The crowd's enjoyment of such eccentric behaviour was not shared by the referee, who promptly added Quiroga's name to those of Manzo, Gorgon and Boniek in his notebook.

Peru: Quiroga, Duarte, Manzo, Chumpitaz, Navarro, Quesada, Cubillas, Cueto, Munante (P. Rojas 45 min.), La Rosa (Sotil 74 min.), Oblitas.

Poland: Kukla, Szymanowski, Gorgon, Zmuda, Maculewicz, Masztaler (Kasperczak 45 min.), Deyna, Boniek (Lubanski 86 min.), Nawalka, Lato, Szarmach (1).

Referee: Pat Partridge (England).

ARGENTINA V BRAZIL

JUNE 18 ROSARIO GROUP B ARGENTINA 0 BRAZIL 0

Imagine Scotland *v* England directed by Sam Peckinpah in Technicolor and Cinemascope, and you will begin to form some impression of the full enormity of this collision. Argentina and Brazil hate the sight of each other – and it showed. Seventeen fouls were committed in the first ten minutes and the match was as unpleasant as it was devoid of goals. Four players were booked – Chicao, Edinho and Zico of Brazil and Villa of Argentina – and Villa could consider himself extremely fortunate to have escaped so lightly after viciously going over the ball to a Brazilian at the start of the second half. It was not so much a crucial World Cup game as a settling of old South American scores.

■ ABOVE AND OPPOSITE. The battle of Rosario: Ardiles and Kempes evade lunging tackles by Batista but Luque is felled
■ INSET. Cesar Luis Menotti: a man burdened with an entire nation's hopes.

Though Argentina could boast the best record of anyone against Brazil in Brazil, they had failed to beat the Brazilians in Argentina for 18 years. Fuel had been heaped on the fire by the rumour, allegedly started by Brazilian journalists, that Mario Kempes had been positively dope-tested after his two-goal spectacular against Poland. Cesar Luis Menotti, the Argentinian manager, said he attached 'scant importance' to the rumours, but the venom was unmistakable when, in answer to a question from a Brazilian journalist about the Brazilian team, Menotti replied: 'Coutinho must have enough problems without another coach analysing the errors made by his team'.

In the event, it was Argentina which started the trouble. With the match but a few minutes old, Luque, restored to full fitness, ran his studs down a Brazilian leg and Bertoni, Kempes and Ardiles were promptly flattened in retaliation. Thankfully, an interlude of eventful football followed. Leao struggled twice to keep Kempes at bay while Fillol managed to thwart Gil once and

Mendonca twice. Then Rodrigues Neto went off injured, his punishment for fouling an opponent, and Edinho came on in time for a close-up of Ortiz missing the best chance of the game by applying too casual a finishing touch to the low centre Bertoni offered him in front of an open goal at the end of a glorious run down the right.

That was just about the end of the legitimate football. The remaining 53 minutes were a succession of fights, injuries, bookings and substitutions. Ardiles was carried off a minute before half time with a sprained ankle and replaced after the interval by the excessively aggressive Villa. Alonso also came on for Ortiz, and Zico for Mendonca, without improving the game as a spectacle. Only in the 72nd minute, when Roberto wasted a good scoring chance created for him by Zico and Batista, was there any further prospect of a goal. At the end of it all, though, Brazil could say that they had successfully shackled Kempes (lying deep again) and that they had picked up another point without the help of Rivelino, a brooding figure on the substitutes' bench.

Argentina: Fillol, Olguin, L. Galvan, Passarella, Tarantino, Ardiles (Villa 45 min.), Gallego, Kempes, Bertoni, Luque, Ortiz (Alonso 60 min.).

Brazil: Leao, Toninho, Oscar, Amaral, Rodrigues Neto (Edinho 34 min.), Chicao, Batista, Dirceu, Gil, Roberto, Mendonca (Zico 67 min.).

Referee: Karoly Palotai (Hungary).

BRAZIL V POLAND

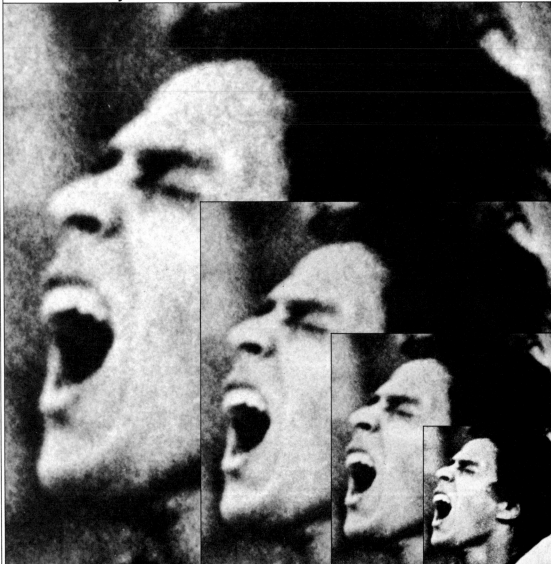

At the beginning of the dénouement in Group B, Brazil must have felt like a foreign boxer on alien soil who knows he has to knock his opponent out to get a draw. Their handicaps were numerous as they set out to beat Poland, no easy task in itself, and qualify for the final of the 1978 World Cup. Having made the long journey back to Mendoza while Argentina rested near Rosario, the Brazilians not only had to win this match but score heavily enough to put pressure on Argentina when they played Peru three-quarters of an hour after the final whistle in Mendoza. The time-lag, like the insistence of FIFA on allowing Argentina to continue with their evening kick-offs, was a scandal. It was argued that, because the population would be at work, Argentina could not draw a crowd in the afternoons. But that was just another way of saying everything must be in the hosts', and television's, favour.

Claudio Coutinho, the Brazilian manager, protested at first. He said, quite reasonably, that it was not fair Argentina should be in the position of knowing exactly what they had to do against Peru. Later, however, he tried to make the best of a bad job by going on the offensive and declaring that, if Brazil scored enough goals, they could make the pressure on Argentina unbearable. It looked as though he could be right, too, when Brazil, pulling out all the stops, played rousingly enough to overcome Poland's spirited resistance by two clear goals. This left Argentina having to beat Peru by four clear goals in order to reach the final.

Poland themselves had not abandoned all hope of meeting Holland in the final. A win against Brazil, a slip by Argentina in the evening and maybe the Poles could make it. No allowance was made, however, for the poorness of the Polish finishing. It had threatened to betray them all through the tournament, and now the threat was carried out. Lato, snatching an equalizer out of chaos in the Brazilian penalty area a minute before half time, took his chance well enough; but sheer carelessness was as responsible as Leao, the Brazilian goal-

keeper, for Poland's failure to score any more goals. Leao was in inspired form throughout, as the frustrated Maculewicz, Deyna, and Lubanski would testify. Yet the match had started so ominously for Brazil, Zico having been carried off after only three minutes following a challenge by Kasperczak. Mendonca came on for him and played a vital role in Brazil's two second half goals. The first of their three, scored after 13 minutes, took some beating. Nelinho proved his recovery from injury complete by swerving a free kick of awesome power and pace into the top corner. If Kukla had got to the ball, it might well have taken him into the net too. But Brazil's real purple patch was between the 58th and 63rd minutes. Roberto scored at each end of that period. He popped in the rebound both times when first Mendonca and then Gil hit a post. Immediately before, Mendonca had already hit the post, and Gil the bar, as a sinuous dribble by Dirceu turned the Polish goal into a shooting gallery. That short fire-storm of classic Brazilian attacking football burned off Poland's remaining hopes of glory. Now, all Brazil could do was sit and wait for the news from Rosario.

Brazil: Leao, Toninho, Oscar, Amaral, Nelinho (1), Cerezo (Rivelino 77 min.), Batista, Dirceu, Gil, Roberto (2), Zico (Mendonca 7 min.).

Poland: Kukla, Szymanowski, Gorgon, Zmuda, Maculewicz, Kasperczak, Deyna, Boniek, Nawalka, Lato (1), Szarmach.

Referee: Juan Silvagno (Chile).

■ ABOVE AND OPPOSITE. Roberto screams in agony.

PERU V ARGENTINA

PERU V ARGENTINA

There are those who will always remain convinced this game was fixed. For all their poor defensive qualities, Peru had not conceded more than three goals in one game previously in the tournament. Indeed, they had only once conceded more than one goal – that when losing 3–0 to a rejuvenated Brazil. Any interpretation you like, too, can be put on the refusal of Marcos Calderon, Peru's manager, to speak to the Pres after the match. What I keep on remembering, though, is the sight o Munante, and then Oblitas, running clean through the Argentinia defence in the early minutes. Munante even contrived to hit a post and it takes extraordinary skill to throw a match with that kind o finesse and precision. It is also worth recalling that the two player booked in the game, both for fouls, were the Peruvians, Quesada and Velasquez. No, it is much more likely that Peru, left with little to play for, were simply overwhelmed on the night by the torrential psycho logical force of a nation on a permanent high.

Once Kempes had exchanged passes beautifully with Luque and put Argentin one up after 21 minutes, it was the Ride of the Valkyrie all over with Wagnerian accompaniment from the 40,000 crowd. Luque hit a post; Orti clipped the bar; Argentina were refused a penalty when Bertoni was brough down; and Passarella came upfield to head a Kempes centre wide. Tense and uncertain, Argentina desperately needed another goal before half time if the were to reach the four-goal target set them by Brazil. But time was running out. Only two minutes of the half remained when Argentina won a corner on the right and Tarantini stooped to head possibly the most important goal of the game.

Peru had begun to kick opponents as well as the ball by the time Kempe made it 3–0 after 51 minutes, but nothing could stop Argentina now. A minut later, Kempes rose at the far post to head the ball down and give the honou of the decisive fourth goal to Luque with his diving header. The fourth and fifth goals were punctuated by a good save by Quiroga from Luque. He mad an even better one from Tarantini later on, and I don't honestly think th affiliations of Peru's Argentina-born goalkeeper can be included in the allegation of a fix. Anyway, back in Quiroga's goalmouth, Houseman scored the fiftl from Ortiz' cross in the 68th minute, a minute after coming on as substitut for Bertoni.

	P	W	D	L	F	A	Pt
ARGENTINA	3	2	1	0	8	0	5
BRAZIL	3	2	1	0	6	1	5
POLAND	3	1	0	2	2	5	2
PERU	3	0	0	3	0	10	0

Significantly, at least for those who believe the match was straight, Rober Wurtz, the French referee, bravely refuse a second Argentinian appeal for a penalt before Luque completed the scoring 1 minutes from the end from a pass by Larrosa, a most impressive deputy i midfield for the injured Ardiles. So, on the first day of winter and on the nigh *Evita* – the musical about Eva Peron, legendary wife of the former Argentinia dictator, Juan Peron – opened in London, Argentina qualified for the final o the World Cup for the first time since the initial tournament, across the Rive Plate in Uruguay, 48 years earlier.

■ PREVIOUS PAGE. How could Peru withstand this pressure? ■ BOTTOM. Quiroga is well beaten by Kempes' first goa
■ TOP. Number four! Argentina reach the final as Luque meets Kempes' headed cross.
■ Effective but illegal: Duarte crash tackles Ortiz ■ INSET. Effective: Kempes throws Quesada off-balance.

Peru: Quiroga, Duarte, Manzo, Chumpitaz, R. Rojas, Velasquez (Gorriti 51 min.), Cubillas, Cueto, Munante, Quesada, Oblitas.
Argentina: Fillol, Olguin, L. Galvan, Passarella, Tarantini (1), Larrosa, Gallego (Oviedo 85 min.), Kempes (2), Bertoni (Houseman 64 min. (1)), Luque (2), Ortiz.
Referee: Robert Wurtz (France).

RON GREENWOOD'S WORLD CUP XI

Picking imaginary teams is a pleasure at the very heart of the fantasies enthusiasts weave around their favourite sport. 'Beat that!' my *Sunday Telegraph* **colleague John Moynihan once said cryptically to a startled Hugh McIlvanney, of the** *Observer,* **as, emerging from the toilet of a Fleet Street pub, he handed him a piece of paper. To his relief McIlvanney discovered on it nothing more challenging than Moynihan's choice of the best England team since the war. Few with an abiding interest in football, I imagine, could deny having fantasized in the same way on numerous occasions. England** *v* **Scotland, Europe** *v* **South America, The World** *v* **Mars. . . . There are no boundaries to this perfect escapist world of the imagination. Guide books abound, though. Journalists covering the 1978 World Cup were asked to nominate their World Cup XI, and every sports magazine in creation must have come out with something similar.**

What we are offering is something slightly different: an expert's World Cup XI. That is not to say football writers are not expert enough in their way; but few,

I am sure, would pretend their knowledge of the game extends as far or goes as deep as that of Ron Greenwood, the England manager. No-one has studied world football with more devotion or insight than he. The brilliant Hungarian team of the early 1950s was his inspiration, and he has always tried to look at and develop English football in the wider context of European and South American trends. He did so during his 13 years as team manager of West Ham United, and he is continuing to do so now that England have finally asked him to give them the benefit of his vast knowledge of the international game.

A FIFA technical adviser at the 1966 and 1970 World Cups and a BBC expert at this one, Greenwood had made up his mind by the end of the second round about the players he would choose in his World Cup XI. The shortage of truly outstanding individuals and the wide range of alternatives for some positions did not make the selection process a simple, straightforward matter; and one had the feeling that Greenwood settled finally for one or two of the names with a certain degree of reluctance. Perhaps some of his choices will cause surprise, even dismay or annoyance. That must be in the nature of things when a World Cup presents so few obvious candidates for glorification. In any case, I have yet to see a 'best' team with which everyone agreed. This, then, is Greenwood's 1978 World Cup XI in 4–3–3 formation and with his reasons for the choice:

Fillol (Argentina)

Vogts (W. Germany)   Oscar (Brazil)   Passarella (Argentina)   Cabrini (Italy)

Ardiles (Argentina)   Platini (France)   Dirceu (Brazil)

Rensenbrink (Holland)   Kempes (Argentina)   Bettega (Italy)

SUBSTITUTES: Zoff (Italy), Krol (Holland), Szymanowski (Poland), Deyna (Poland), Rossi (Italy).

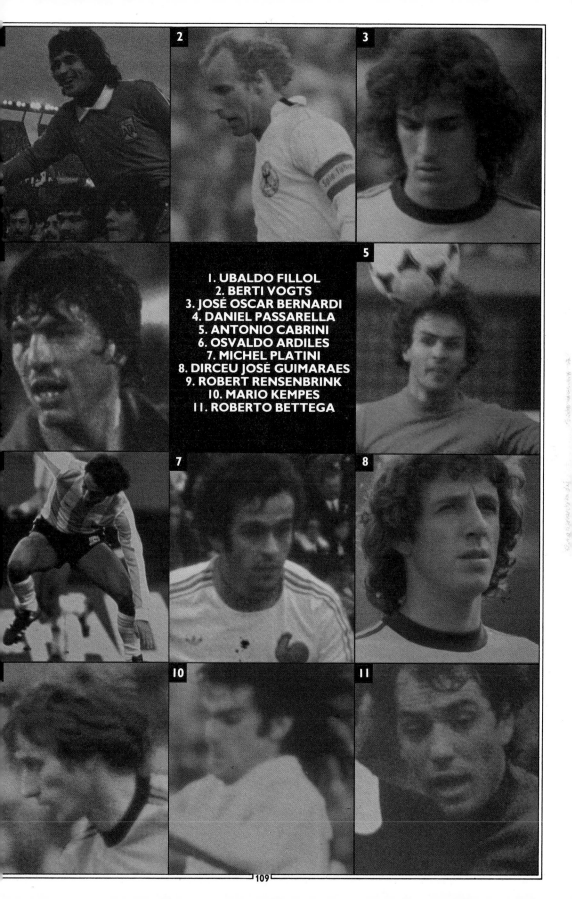

1. UBALDO FILLOL
2. BERTI VOGTS
3. JOSÉ OSCAR BERNARDI
4. DANIEL PASSARELLA
5. ANTONIO CABRINI
6. OSVALDO ARDILES
7. MICHEL PLATINI
8. DIRCEU JOSÉ GUIMARAES
9. ROBERT RENSENBRINK
10. MARIO KEMPES
11. ROBERTO BETTEGA

Ron Greenwood's World Cup XI

Ubaldo Fillol (Age 27 *River Plate*)★

'I was going to have Dino Zoff as my goalkeeper until he let two in from outside the box against Holland. Fillol is probably the steadier of the two. He did no concede a single goal in the second round. Fillol is an unspectacular 'keeper but he gets his angles right, comes out well and has a good command of his area Because he hasn't got a big defence in front of him, he has to deal with the high centres himself. He's agile and he reads the game well – which is very importan now that goalkeepers must be second full backs.'

Berti Vogts (Age 31 *Borussia Mönchengladbach*)

'Though Vogts is not a particularly inspiring captain, he always senses dange at the right time. That sixth sense was responsible for the two great inter ceptions he made against Italy. He is an excellent man-to-man marker, yet h can defend zonally just as well. He also makes an attacking contribution – th first of West Germany's six goals against Mexico was made by Vogts. He's worker, a down-to-earth player who reads situations well. Vogts is two-footed and quick, but above all he's experienced.'

José Oscar Bernardi 'Oscar' (Age 23 *Ponte Preta*)

'You have got to have a stopper, and Oscar would be my choice. He is a mobil player who gets through his work simply. You don't notice him much becaus of that, but he is good in the air and uses the ball well. The smaller type of centr forward is sometimes a problem for a big man like Oscar, but I have seen hin adapt well to such an opponent. He's quick into the tackle and quick to recover Perhaps his biggest attribute is that he can mark space. He doesn't have to hav someone to mark: he can almost play "loose".'

Daniel Passarella (Age 25 *River Plate*)

'I had terrible trouble deciding between Passarella and Krol for the position o sweeper. Krol is the steadier of the two, but I went for Passarella in the enc because he is a bit more adventurous than the Dutch skipper. I see Argentina' captain as a good example of the modern, athletic player. He's fit and aggressive quick and mobile, he's got a great left stick and he uses the ball well.'

Antonio Cabrini (Age 20 *Juventus*)

'This choice will probably surprise a few, though I understand Enzo Bearzo has already caused the major surprise by picking Cabrini for Italy when h wasn't even in the Juventus first team. I can understand Enzo's liking for th boy. He's quick and mobile, and he comes forward well and he marks peopl really tight. The great thing about Cabrini is that he has got lots of tim ahead of him. So he could develop into a really great left back.'

Osvaldo Ardiles (Age 25 *Huracán*)

'An outstanding player. He comes forward and supports others well, he's a fighte who battles hard in midfield and he plays great balls wide. In fact, Ardiles i one of those players who seems to be all over the place. He created a beautifu goal for Kempes against Poland. He went the full length of the pitch in tha move. Two-footed and quick, Ardiles is always making himself available for th ball, and I can imagine him and Dirceu interchanging in midfield without stress.

Ron Greenwood's World Cup XI

Michel Platini (Age 22 *Nancy*)

'This chap is going to be a star of the future, I am absolutely convinced of it. I don't think we saw the best of him in this World Cup. His long-range shooting is tremendous, and he has amazing skill for one so young He always gives himself space and time to do things, and he created some wonderful chances for France. Their downfall was that they did not have someone to stick the ball away regularly. Ardiles and Dirceu would be wonderful foils for Platini because he is not quite as hardworking as they are. But he has a bit more style. Like Bobby Charlton and Trevor Brooking, he has got that ability to look cool and unhurried under pressure. His range of passes and shots is amazing, and he has that hallmark of the great player – eyes in the back of the head.'

Dirceu José Guimaraes 'Dirceu' (Age 25 *Vasco da Gama*)

'A natural left foot on the left-hand side of the field is always a bonus, and Dirceu has a beauty. A busy midfield player, he works up and down that left flank like a Trojan and he doesn't mind finding himself in wide positions. To tell you the truth, he reminds me a lot of the young Alan Ball: he has that extra bit of zip in his play. Blessed with a beautiful touch and a wide range of vision, Dirceu is also very tenacious. In other words, he is a complete all-rounder.'

Robert Rensenbrink (Age 30 *Anderlecht*)

'I preferred Rensenbrink to Lato and Causio as my outside right mainly because he can score goals. The Dutchman not only has a lot of skill, he knows where the goal is. With him alongside Kempes and Bettega, you would have three proven goalscorers in attack. He wouldn't be averse to playing on the right, I'm sure, because he murdered us (West Ham) down that side in the 1976 European Cup Winners Cup final. Rensenbrink has many qualities as a player. He can take people on or hold up the ball until others come in support. Smooth and graceful, thin and wiry, he looks so much like Cruyff at times it's uncanny.'

Mario Kempes (Age 23 *Valencia*)

'Kempes is not an orthodox centre forward. He can go past people on the right or left and he knows where the goal is, but he has also got the ability to roam out of position without feeling unhappy. The way he plays is the sort of thing we have been trying in the England team with Kevin Keegan and Trevor Francis. Hard to mark and good at making chances for others, Kempes gives you the feeling that something is going to happen whenever he gets the ball. I think he would work very well with Bettega, because the Italian needs someone to make space for his blind-side runs into the goalmouth. Kempes would do that.'

Roberto Bettega (Age 27 *Juventus*)

'Bettega has that wonderful ability to attack the ball in the box that Poland's Szarmach showed in West Germany four years ago, but not here. He wants to score goals, and that is a very important part of a goal scorer's make-up. He must be a nice player to play with in a build-up, because he is so uncomplicated. He's almost a one-touch player, since he is quite willing to give it and go. Bettega senses that it is not his job to take people on but to get into the box. There he is very cool, and deadly in the air. The possessor of a good left foot and shot, Bettega can also be useful defensively.' * At start of World Cup in all cases.

Ron Greenwood's World Cup XI

Dino Zoff (Age 36 *Juventus*)

'Until he was caught a bit flat on his line by Holland, I thought Zoff was the most accomplished goalkeeper in the finals. His great experience would be an asset to any side.'

Ruud Krol (Age 29 *Ajax Amsterdam*)

'As I have said, there was little to choose between him and Passarella. Krol is a delightful player with plenty of experience, and he could provide cover in more than one position at the back.'

Antoni Szymanowski (Age 27 *Wisla Krakow*)

'Despite Krol's versatility, you would need a specialist full back. I choose Szymanowski because he is a battler who is always in the thick of things. He comes forward well, and only greater experience put Berti Vogts ahead of him in my estimation.'

Kazimierz Deyna (Age 30 *Legia Warsaw*)

'Deyna is a wonderful general with a lot of experience. Though he probably did not have as good a World Cup as four years ago, he would fill in anywhere along the middle line and do a good job.'

Paolo Rossi (Age 21 *Lanerossi Vicenza*)

'Rossi really emerged in this World Cup. Very quick and bright, he is happy to go on the wings and leave the centre forward spot for others to exploit. He is good at setting up things for others. Definitely a star of the future, this boy.'

12. DINO ZOFF
13. RUUD KROL
14. ANTONI SZYMANOWSKI
15. KAZIMIERZ DEYNA
16. PAOLO ROSSI

MARIO ALBERTO KEMPES

OUTSTANDING PLAYER OF THE TOURNAMENT

full flight, with long, black hair wing behind him, mpes was really nething to be- d." –Ron Green- od.

Like the rest of us, Greenwood did not have to look far for his outstand-ng player of the 1978 World Cup finals. Even before Mario Kempes had dominated the final itself, it was clear there could be no other choice but Argentina's dark, avenging angel. In the end, he not only scored more goals than anyone else, but upstaged all rivals comprehensively. t was not just a question of exquisite balance, speed of foot and power of shot – though Kempes had them all: no-one else could match the sheer dramatic effect of the man. As Greenwood said of him: 'In full flight, with his long, black hair flowing behind him, Kempes was really something to behold. South Americans tend to have the edge on Europeans in flair

Mario Alberto Kempes

and flamboyance, and Kempes was certainly miles ahead of any European in this tournament.' The Argentinian led a field not up to the standards of 1970 and 1974, admittedly – but he was so far out in front there is little doubt he could have held his own with the best.

Kempes is nothing if not versatile. Cesar Luis Menotti, Argentina's manager, played him in three different positions and he excelled in all of them. Starting as a striker to the left of Luque, Kempes moved to centre forward when his attacking partner was injured and then he dropped deeper when Luque returned so that Ortiz could continue on the left wing. His devastating partnership with Luque was the talk of the first round; but it wasn't until Luque was injured that Kempes started scoring. 'He was at his best without Luque,' asserts Greenwood. 'He is certainly a better player than Luque: he has got more control.' Nevertheless, the understanding between them was quite remarkable considering they had not played together before the 1978 World Cup. Kempes, born in Cordoba, left the Rosario Central club in 1976 to join the Spanish club Valencia, while Luque remained with the River Plate club in Buenos Aires. Then Kempes did not return until a month before the finals. 'Somehow, we just clicked immediately,' said Kempes. 'I can't explain why. It just happened. When Leopoldo was injured against France, I missed him in the next two matches. He helps me a great deal. He's a fighter and he is always battling for the ball. If he hasn't got it, he goes looking for it. I think I am best suited to a role just behind the main attackers. That's how I've been playing in Spain (where he was Valencia's top scorer in his first two seasons), and Menotti knew it. For me, there were no difficulties in joining the Argentina squad. I've kept in touch with Argentinian football through newspapers and magazines, and friends and other Argentinian footballers are always coming to Spain.'

These were Kempes' second World Cup finals. After equalizing for Argentina with a last-minute penalty in the 2–2 draw with England at Wembley, in 1974 he went to West Germany as a promising, 19-year old striker. There, however, he was overshadowed by Rene Houseman, Miguel Brindisi and Carlos Babington. More maturity was required, and it came to him at Valencia. 'I think I pace my game better now after playing in Europe. When I was younger, I used to waste too much energy early in the game. After about 75 minutes I'd blow up. I can conserve energy more now because I read situations better. I enjoy playing for Valencia because they are an attacking team, and I have revelled in Argentina's adventurous style because it enables me to be in the game all the time. Argentina's aim was to go out and win every match by as many goals as possible. The defenders and midfield men put opponents under tremendous pressure, and we always had a lot of possession.'

At times, Kempes sounds almost too good to be true. By agreeing to sign a new five-year contract with Valencia just before he left for Argentina – a very shrewd move by the Spanish club, as it turns out – the man who is now probably the most famous and admired footballer in the world has done himself out of a small fortune. With the reputation he acquired in the World Cup finals, Kempes could have named his own price to the richest clubs in the world. Yet he insists: 'I am happy with Valencia. Though we didn't win anything last season, we've got some new players now and I'm optimistic about our chances. Perhaps I could earn more elsewhere, but money doesn't necessarily buy happiness.' If Kempes is sincere, then football might have found itself something really unusual in the way of idols.

ITALY V BRAZIL

JUNE 24 BUENOS AIRES THIRD & FOURTH PLACE ITALY 1 BRAZIL 2

Usually, this celebration of failure is about as much fun as a funeral. More often than not, the players are preoccupied with their own gloomy reflections on what might have been, and they rarely show much interest in the rather meaningless ritual of deciding who comes third and fourth in the World Cup. Not so this time. Shaking off their fatigue and the inevitable sense of anti-climax, Italy and Brazil disputed the consolation prize with a degree of determination and commitment which made this the most enjoyable Third Place Match for a long time - enjoyable, that is, for all but Italy.

am convinced that the best football this World Cup was played by y."—Enzo Bearzot.

Once again, they allowed themselves to be overtaken in the second half after leading 1–0 at half time. So the Italians had to go home empty-handed, a poor reward for their astonishing change of character and fine, attacking contribution to this World Cup. Many echoed the words of their manager, Enzo Bearzot, when he said afterwards: 'I believe Italy deserved better luck in this championship. I am convinced that the best football in this World Cup was played by Italy.'

Bettega, certainly, was unlucky when he headed against the bar in the last minute, and Italy definitely played a lot better than Brazil in the first half. Even without what had become their first choice midfield – Tardelli, Benetti and Zaccarelli – Italy displayed the more urgent rhythm and greater collective strength. As Antognoni sent two shots whizzing at Leao's goal inside the first minute and Patrizio Sala and Maldera made life difficult for Brazil's midfield, it seemed the suspensions collected by Tardelli and Benetti for two bookings each might not have been insuperable problems had Italy qualified for the final.

That feeling swelled considerably when Italy nearly scored three times in the last seven minutes of the half. They did, in fact, score once, Causio heading in at the far post in the 38th minute after Rossi had cheekily shown Amaral the ball on the right and then dummied past him. In the hectic scenes that followed, Causio hit the bar when Leao was unable to hold successive shots from Patrizio Sala and Rossi, and the effervescent Rossi drove a shot against the outside of a post from a narrow angle after running on to Cuccureddu's gorgeous through pass and rounding Leao.

Cuccureddu, of course, was playing because Bellugi was still troubled by the injury which had kept him out of the game against Holland. Yet it was not until early in the second half, when Cuccureddu was very fortunate to get away with a foul on Mendonca in the Italian penalty area, that signs of stress were visible in the Italian defence. Stress became collapse, however, when Nelinho suddenly caught Zoff napping after 64 minutes with one of his immensely powerful, but outrageously optimistic shots. He hit it from out near the right-wing corner flag and the ball wobbled several different ways in the air after taking a deflection off Bettega.

■ Emerson Leao looks apprehensive but his luck, especially in the first half, held out.

Italy V Brazil

Fate had not finished with Zoff. His torture from long range continued when Dirceu, who had again proved himself the new maestro of Brazil's midfield suddenly smashed a volley into the Italian net from outside the penalty area to emphasize his team's sharper sense of purpose in the second half. The old maestro, Rivelino, came on right after that goal for a farewell to World Cup football which reminded us that, at his peak, he was both bandit and poet. It was good, too, to have a rare look at Reinaldo, the gifted youngster whose career has been blighted by continual cartilage trouble.

So Brazil, in danger of elimination in the first round, eventually finished third and unbeaten. And the achievement provided a platform for this final personal statement by the beleagured and long-suffering Brazilian manager, Claudio Coutinho: 'What is really important is that Brazil today defeated an attacking completely renewed football team. With this victory it closes an excellent performance. I am sure the Brazilian people, or at least part of them who know how to value our efforts, will bear in mind this magnificent demonstration of technique and discipline. Maybe some fans may not share my opinion, but I believe that we have given no cause for reproach since this third place in the World Cup is clear evidence of a good performance.'

Italy: Zoff, Cuccureddu, Gentile, Scirea, Cabrini, P. Sala, Antognoni (C. Sala 78 min.), Maldera, Causio (1), Rossi, Bettega.
Brazil: Leao, Nelinho (1), Oscar, Amaral, Rodrigues Neto, Cerezo (Rivelino 64 min.), Batista, Dirceu (1), Gil (Reinaldo 45 min.), Roberto, Mendonca.
Referee: Abraham Klein (Israel).

■ From start to finish a fine match despite Cerezo's bodycheck on Maldera. Causio scores Italy's goal but although Italy lose two it handshakes and exchanges all round.

FINAL

Final

Where to start? Though severely disappointing in many ways, the fin⟨al⟩ of the 1978 World Cup was, without question, one of *the* great occasio⟨ns⟩ in the history of the competition. It could hardly be anything else whi⟨le⟩ the River Plate remained an active volcano spewing out sizzling rive⟨rs⟩ of blue and white lava. In its depths, the emotional heat was almo⟨st⟩ unbearable. My abiding memory of the day will always be the sig⟨ht⟩ and sound of my urbane Argentinian neighbour vomiting his nervo⟨us⟩ tension on to the floor of the Press box when Mario Kempes scored h⟨is⟩ second goal to put Argentina 2–1 up in extra time. *That* is how mu⟨ch⟩ winning the World Cup for the first time meant to the people ⟨of⟩ Argentina.

Unfortunately, the team stooped to conquer. The proximity of the major pri⟨ze⟩ caused a recrudescence of that nasty, provocative streak in Argentinian footb⟨all⟩ which had been heavily disguised for most of the tournament. In a crud⟨e,⟩ distasteful attempt to put psychological pressure on Holland, Argentina kept t⟨he⟩ Dutchmen waiting for five minutes in the bedlam outside before deigning ⟨to⟩ make the entrance that should have coincided with that of their opponen⟨ts.⟩ Then they held up the kick-off by complaining about the small plaster cast ⟨on⟩ Rene Van der Kerkhof's right hand.

Not a single opponent in Holland's previous five matches had objected to t⟨he⟩ cast Van der Kerkhof had worn to protect an injury sustained in his countr⟨y's⟩ opening World Cup game. So the last-minute protest was obviously a lit⟨tle⟩ dirty trick Argentina had been saving up. More alarming still, the Italian refer⟨ee,⟩ Sergio Gonella, seemed prepared to take it seriously. So much so that, at o⟨ne⟩ point, the Dutch threatened to walk off the field and out of the final altogethe⟨r.⟩ In the end, Van der Kerkhof was allowed to wear the cast with a soft cover ov⟨er⟩ it; but the damage to the match had been done. Signor Gonella, a compromi⟨se⟩ choice when the FIFA Referees Committee could not agree on the man ⟨to⟩ control the final, had been thoroughly discredited before a ball was kicke⟨d⟩ and Holland – never the gentlest of teams – had been put in an ominous⟨ly⟩ ugly and vengeful mood. That much was clear from the way Poortvliet a⟨nd⟩ Haan chopped down Bertoni and Ardiles in the first three minutes.

It became even clearer as Dutch aggression was met by Argentinian slyne⟨ss⟩ and as Signor Gonella adopted a wholly inconsistent attitude to the recurri⟨ng⟩ misbehaviour. During the two hours of play, the referee booked three Dutchme⟨n,⟩ Krol, Poortvliet and Suurbier, and one Argentinian, Ardiles; and the ratio w⟨as⟩ just about right on balance. Yet he also ignored completely a blatant bod⟨y⟩ check off the ball by Passarella on Neeskens and failed to punish adequate⟨ly⟩ repeated cases of deliberate hand-ball by Argentina.

Mercifully, Signor Gonella's dreadful refereeing had no direct bearing on t⟨he⟩ result. His susceptibility to the play-acting of the Argentinians, who fell in⟨to⟩ their old habit of feigning injury, must have irritated Holland beyond measur⟨e;⟩ but it was Mario Kempes who beat them. Without him, Argentina would ha⟨ve⟩ been a quite ordinary team. Without him, Argentina would not have won t⟨he⟩ World Cup. He was, as Johan Neeskens was to say later: 'a very great player, ⟨at⟩ least 50 per cent of his team'.

For a long time, the other 50 per cent appeared to be Ubaldo Fillol. Argentina⟨'s⟩ steadily-improving goalkeeper made two miraculous saves in the first half to de⟨ny⟩

■ OVER. The pain and the power: Tarantini and Luque take the brunt but Fillol saves Neeskens' free kick ■ INSETS. Tim⟨e to⟩ win, time to lose: Neeskens and Nanninga rejoice: Gallego is horror-struck ■ Neeskens' header goes wide.

118

Rep and Rensenbrink what looked to be certain goals as the host nation persisted in giving the ball away and as Holland found ways and means of overcoming their opponents' attempted use of the offside trap. A case in point was the Haan free kick that Rep, climbing above the diminutive Argentinian defence, squandered badly by heading wide after only 16 minutes. To an extent, therefore, Holland beat themselves.

They gave every appearance of making a conscious effort to do so by twice allowing Passarella to materialize dangerously on the blind side of their defence. Like Passarella, Bertoni lost his head when in the clear; and, by and large, Holland's man-to-man marking – Poortvliet on Bertoni, Brandts on Luque, Jansen on Ortiz and Willy Van der Kerkhof on Kempes – worked well until Ardiles managed to engineer an attack on the left after 38 minutes.

A square pass by Luque and momentary hesitation by the Dutch defence was all Kempes needed to break through the protective wall around Jongbloed and squeeze the ball into the Dutch net. The goal was like a sudden flash of lightning on a thundery summer's day, but it galvanized Holland rather than Argentina. Fillol was again under heavy fire in the early stages of the second half, and only Kempes' occasional raids kept Argentina's spirits up. Four substitutions, two by each team, were made as the rivals fought to control the game in the last half hour of normal time, and the vital change proved to be that of Nanninga for Rep.

The tall striker did exactly what had been expected of him by heading the equalizer at the far post eight minutes from the end when Haan's beautiful pass put Rene Van der Kerkhof clear on the right for a telling centre. Jan Zwartkruis, Holland's assistant manager, had warned that Holland would open the eyes of the Argentinian crowd to the mistakes their heroes were making as they tried to play alien, European-style football. It sounded more like a prophecy than a warning as Krol's long free kick suddenly caught the Argentinian defence hopelessly out of position in the very last minute of normal time.

Rensenbrink, that stealthy infiltrator of defences, sneaked around the outside of an opponent to flick at the ball with the outside of his foot. The angle was too narrow for him, however, and the shot cannoned away to safety off the outside of the relieved Fillol's right-hand post. Argentina could not have complained if the ball had gone in. At that point, Holland, better-organized, more experienced and generally more effective, would have been worthy winners.

The first half of extra time was mainly an exchange of fouls until Bertoni put Kempes through in the same inside left position from which he had scored his first goal. Jongbloed came out fast, but could only half block the shot, and two other Dutchmen failed to clear the rebound instantly. That was a scoring invitation to a player as quick and accurate as Kempes, and he accepted it with delight. Holland felt Kempes had enjoyed more than his fair share of luck because all the bounces had gone his way; but it was largely the old, old story of a great player making his own luck.

Whatever the rights and wrongs of the case, Kempes was now the highest scorer in the 1978 World Cup with six goals and Argentina had built up sufficient confidence and momentum to win it. In the second half of extra time, and for the first time in the match, Cesar's army charged forward with all the old self-belief. Menotti had seriously doubted his players' capacity to match the speed,

■ OVER. The joy and the horror: Kempes scores the second despite Poortvliet and Brandts and Kempes dances off towards the World Cup ■ INSETS. Menotti and Videla: to whom does Argentina owe most?

application and stamina of the Europeans, but here they were proving him wrong again.

Houseman sent the ball into the side-netting and Jongbloed barely saved from the runaway Luque before Kempes finally put Holland out of their misery by running at the heart of their defence and playing a double one-two with Bertoni. There was a suspicion of offside as Bertoni wriggled clear to shoot past Jongbloed, but referees a lot braver than Signor Gonella would have suddenly gone blind in one eye in that situation. Buenos Aires was about to go mad, and only a fool would have stood in the way.

The youngsters selling Coca-Cola, so polite and restrained throughout the tournament, were now jumping up and down in the aisles of the Press box like dervishes, grim-faced policemen were smiling under funny hats and wearing the Argentinian flag like a shawl and the whole of Buenos Aires – indeed the whole of Argentina – was beginning to grind to a halt. For hours afterwards, the country was one big hooting, honking, yelling, screaming, singing traffic jam.

One man had made it all possible. I do not refer to President Videla, champion of 'law and order', whose national team had not played fair when it mattered, but to the much more influential Mario Kempes. In the final the man was a colossus. In one breathtaking run he hurdled three or four savage Dutch attempts to cut him down with an ease and a contempt which stamped him as a very special player. Equally impressive was the calming influence Kempes exerted on friend and foe alike when tempers ran high. For God's sake, the man turned out to be a diplomat, too!

I think it is fair to say Holland would have destroyed Argentina if they had had Kempes. Not only because of his skill but because of his leadership. Holland have now lost twice in the World Cup final and I am beginning to believe their suspect temperament is chiefly to blame. All too readily, they lose control of their feelings and allow themselves to be thrown out of their stride. In fact, they over-react to situations like Scotsmen with the blood up.

It is a serious flaw in an otherwise admirable attitude to, and thrilling mastery of, the game. At the end of this World Cup managers were still talking about the Dutch. Enzo Bearzot summed it all up for us when he said: 'I think Holland play the best football in the world. However, it was believed in 1974 that Holland were unbeatable. Today that is no longer the case. All these remarks refer to performance. As regards a result, anybody can win.'

Argentina: Fillol, Olguin, L. Galvan, Passarella, Tarantini, Ardiles (Larrosa 66 min.), Gallego, Kempes (2), Bertoni (1), Luque, Ortiz (Houseman 75 min.).
Holland: Jongbloed, Jansen (Suurbier 73 min.), Krol, Brandts, Poortvliet, W. Van der Kerkhof, Neeskens, Haan, R. Van der Kerkhof, Rep (Nanninga 60 min., (1)), Rensenbrink.
Referee: Sergio Gonella (Italy).

■ Johnny Rep sums up Dutch opinions of Sergio Gonella, the Italian referee.

BETTER THAN EXPECTED

Considerably better than expected: that must be the final verdict on Argentina '78. Double hernias be damned! This much-maligned World Cup turned out to have all the capacity to delight of an expensive surprise present. Despite the scarcity of established stars, there was no shortage of entertaining football or of goals; until the final, the notorious Argentinian footballers were on their best behaviour; one or two referees did have the courage to resist the intimidation of Argentinian crowds and, overall, the standard of refereeing was not too bad; the world game acquired a new and worthy standard bearer in Mario Kempes; terrorism did not – or was not allowed to – intrude; after a sticky start, the organization of the tournament functioned very smoothly; and, above all, there was the extreme friendliness of the Argentinian people.

If you see a contradiction in that paragraph you have read it thoroughly. The Argentinians *are* extremely friendly people : yet their football crowds *do* intimidate referees and their footballers *are* inclined to stop opponents by foul means.

"The increase in pressure seems continuous from one competition to the next. In 1966 it was already terrific, in 1970 it was worse, in 1974 still more terrible and now it is almost completely out of hand."—Helmut Schön.

In fact, the Argentinian national character is one giant paradox. Joao Saldanha, the journalist, broadcaster and former manager of Brazil, remarked upon it by contrasting the nastiness of Argentinians inside a football stadium with their solicitous rush to help an old lady to her feet should she fall in the street.

Not that we saw much nastiness anywhere during June, 1978 in Argentina. The kindness and helpfulness had to be experienced to be believed. On my first day in the country, a Sunday, a complete stranger gave me and some other journalists a 1000 peso note (approximately 70p) so that we could get across Buenos Aires to the Press Centre to change travellers cheques. It was, he insisted, a gift not a loan. When you asked people in the street for directions, they would not just tell you and leave it at that: they actually went out of their way to lead you personally to your destination. On one occasion, too, a taxi driver even refused payment when he discovered his passenger was an English journalist.

That, I might add, was all in Buenos Aires, a huge, sprawling, sophisticated metropolis with claims for inclusion among the great cities of the world. So you can imagine, perhaps, the scale of the reception for foreign visitors out in the more naive and open-hearted provinces. Cordoba was an absolute revelation. The citizens would stand and gawp at you unself-consciously as though seeing beings from another planet. Stand and gawp, that is, when they were not clustering around foreigners, whatever their status in the football hierarchy, and asking for autographs.

One theory was that, between them, the insatiable curiosity of the people of Cordoba and the wearing of official and semi-official uniforms and shirts by Scotland's camp-followers were responsible for many of the wildly exaggerated stories about the players' drinking habits. In other words, intoxicated fans and others were mistaken for players. That may, or may not, be true. There was no doubt, however, that the Argentinians really put themselves out to make their visitors welcome. To what extent the hospitality was genuine and spontaneous

Better than expected

it was difficult to judge. For the population was constantly being exhorted by government propaganda to behave correctly and present its best face to the world. But it is hard to believe that it was all the result of brainwashing.

Clearly, though, some of it was. Mindful of the spread of soccer hooliganism over their own continent, European journalists marvelled at the total absence of fighting and vandalism from the deafening, mind-blowing celebrations during and after every match of Argentina's. Yet it was not always so. Before the World Cup rival supporters were clashing just as bitterly as ours in Britain; and one wondered how long the good behaviour would last once Argentina '78 was over and done with, once the festive feeling of national unity had been eroded by time and politics.

That consideration, I suspect, was less important to the junta than the fact that the 1978 World Cup had served its immediate purpose. By proving they could stage a smooth, trouble-free tournament and by identifying with it constantly, President Videla's government cannot have failed to impress those foreigners who ever contemplated investing capital in Argentina. They did it subtly, too. Uniforms were kept to a minimum, and one was conscious of being surrounded by far fewer police and soldiers than in West Germany four years earlier, though there were probably just as many, if not more.

Despite all the hidden security, bomb stories abounded. Four more were rumoured to have been found in the Buenos Aires Press Centre and removed successfully this time. Official confirmation was hard to come by, but the *Buenos Aires Herald* reported on June 22nd that three bombs had exploded in Buenos Aires the night before. One, a pamphlet bomb, showered a street with leaflets carrying the slogan: 'Argentina Champion – Videla to the Wall!', and another was thought to have gone off in the region of the Army General Command building. The third, however, was less obviously the work of terrorists. It damaged the home of Juan Alemann, the Treasury Secretary, who criticized the high cost of holding the World Cup in Argentina.

Nevertheless, there was never in Argentina the sense of dread and impending disaster one experiences uneasily in, say, Belfast. The moving demonstrations by the 'Mad Mothers of the Plaza de Mayo', as they called themselves, to draw attention to the unexplained disappearance of their children and close relatives were a weekly reminder of the political troubles just below the surface of Argentinian society. Equally disturbing was the disappearance, and subsequent death, of a local newspaper editor; but, Argentinian friends of mine kept insisting, life was a lot more precarious before the military had taken over. We were, of course, in no position to judge whether or not that was true.

A few of the football managers, I imagine, would not have objected too strongly to being abducted. The pressures on them in this World Cup were so intense that almost anything else would have been blessed release from the fear of failure, the endless round of press conferences and the internecine warfare. Scarcely any of the 16 camps was completely free from trouble of one kind or another, and the managers hastening to make it quite clear their contracts ended with the World Cup were legion. Television and newspaper pictures brought into sharp focus the suffering of a group of men on the rack of professional pride, personal ambition and nationalism.

Inevitably, there were anomalies. Claudio Coutinho, a marked man from the moment Brazil drew their first two matches, is no longer that country's manager even though they finished third and were the only team not to lose a single

Better than expected

match. Ally MacLeod, on the other hand, received a truly astonishing vote of confidence from the Scottish Football Association, who blamed their three 'black sheep', Willie Johnston, Don Masson and Lou Macari, and the media for Scotland's elimination in the first round. That was rather like holding the horses responsible for the Charge of the Light Brigade, and Scotland can expect little sympathy from the world at large should their international results take another turn for the worse.

There was, however, a note of fellow feeling in the illuminating and disturbing interview Helmut Schön, the retiring West German doyen of the game, gave to Hugh McIlvanney of *The Observer* towards the end of Argentina '78. 'The World Cups of 1958 and 1962 were garden parties compared with what is involved now, with the pressures that have developed,' said Schön. 'The increase in pressure seems continuous from one competition to the next. In 1966 it was already terrific, in 1970 it was worse, in 1974 still more terrible and now it is almost completely out of hand.

'In nearly all the countries of the world, football is the most popular sport, and today the media bring it to the masses and bring the feelings and demands of the masses back to those working in the game. Football has become almost a kind of war. It is my great fear that one day, perhaps soon, the World Cup will no longer be the sporting event that you and I have enjoyed and competed in. It may all become too big, too important, too hard on the people concerned, just impossible to go on with . . . it is crazy for people in FIFA to talk of increasing the number of competing countries in the finals to as many as 24. That is madness.'

It certainly is. While FIFA were blithely discussing at their congress the possibility of inflating the tournament still further in Spain in 1982 and in Colombia four years later, there was nearly a riot at the Press Centre elsewhere in Buenos Aires as thousands of journalists struggled to get tickets to cover the matches of just 16 finalists. As Helmut Schön says, the World Cup has become too big, too serious and too self-important, not to mention prohibitively expensive. FIFA should be thinking in terms of reduction, not increase. Eight finalists competing over a fortnight would be the ideal World Cup.

I speak as a sports writer, of course, just as Schön represents another comparatively powerless body of men, the football managers. The people who wield the real influence in this context are the television companies. Their bottomless purses will decide how many finalists there will be at future World Cups. If television wants 24 teams it will get 24 teams whether the host country likes it or not. FIFA won't argue because the continuing spread of the game, in the Third World and America particularly, means more countries than ever will want to compete. By the time World Cup 2002 comes along, perhaps they will have to hire Africa, set a whole year aside and put a bulk order for straitjackets out to tender. I hope not, but without any great conviction.

■ Nanninga equalizes and in Amsterdam they celebrate before the television screen.

PLAYERS & OFFICIALS

ARGENTINA

Goalkeepers	3	Hector Baley	*Huracán*
	5	Ubaldo Fillol	*River Plate*
	13	Ricardo Lavolpe	*San Lorenzo Alm*
Defenders	7	Luis Galvan	*Talleres (CBA)*
	11	Daniel Killer	*Racing Club*
	15	Jorge Olguin	*SL de Almagro*
	17	Miguel Oviedo	*Talleres (Cordoba)*
	18	Ruben Pagnanini	*Independiente*
	19	Daniel Passarella	*River Plate*
	20	Alberto Tarantini	*AFA*
Midfield	1	Norberto Alonso	*River Plate*
	2	Osvaldo Ardiles	*Huracán*
	6	Americo Gallego	*Newell's Old Boys*
	8	Ruben Galvan	*Independiente*
	12	Omar Larrosa	*Independiente*
	21	Daniel Valencia	*Talleres (CBA)*
	22	Ricardo Villa	*Racing Club*
Forwards	4	Daniel Bertoni	*Independiente*
	9	Rene Houseman	*Huracán*
	10	Mario Kempes	*Valencia FC (Spain)*
	14	Leopoldo Luque	*River Plate*
	16	Oscar Ortiz	*River Plate*

Manager Cesar Luis Menotti

FRANCE

Goalkeepers	1	Dominique Baratelli	*Nice*
	21	Jean-Paul Bertrand-Demanes	*Nantes*
	22	Dominique Dropsy	*Strasbourg*
Defenders	2	Patrick Battiston	*Metz*
	3	Maxime Bossis	*Nantes*
	4	Gerard Janvion	*Saint-Etienne*
	5	François Bracci	*Marseille*
	6	Christian Lopez	*Saint-Etienne*
	7	Patrice Rio	*Nantes*
	8	Marius Tresor	*Marseille*
Midfield	9	Dominique Bathenay	*Saint-Etienne*
	10	Jean-Marc Guillou	*Nice*
	11	Henri Michel	*Nantes*
	12	Claude Papi	*Bastia*
	13	Jean Petit	*Monaco*
	15	Michel Platini	*Nancy*
Forwards	14	Marc Berdoll	*Marseille*
	16	Christian Dalger	*Monaco*
	17	Bernard Lacombe	*Lyon*
	18	Dominique Rocheteau	*Saint-Etienne*
	19	Didier Six	*Lens*
	20	Olivier Rouyer	*Nancy*

Manager Michel Hidalgo

AUSTRIA

Goalkeepers	1	Friedl Koncilia	*Wacker Innsbruck*
	21	Erwin Fuchsbichler	*VOEST Linz*
	22	Hubert Baumgartner	*Austria Wien*
Defenders	2	Robert Sara	*Austria Wien*
	3	Erich Obermayer	*Austria Wien*
	4	Gerhard Breitenberger	*VOEST Linz*
	5	Bruno Pezzey	*Wacker Innsbruck*
	12	Edi Kreiger	*FC Brugge*
	13	Günther Happich	*Wiener Sport Club*
	14	Heinrich Strasser	*Admira/Wacker*
	16	Peter Persidis	*Rapid Wien*
Midfield	6	Roland Hattenberger	*VfB Stuttgart*
	7	Josef Hickersberger	*Fortuna Düsseldorf*
	8	Herbert Prohaska	*Austria Wien*
	11	Kurt Jara	*MSV Duisburg*
	15	Heribert Weber	*Sturm Graz*
	20	Ernst Baumeister	*Austria Wien*
Forwards	9	Johan Krankl	*Rapid Wien*
	10	Willy Kreuz	*Feyenoord (Rotterdam)*
	17	Franz Oberacher	*Wacker Innsbruck*
	18	Walter Schachner	*SV Donawitz*
	19	Hans Pirkner	*Austria Wien*

Manager Helmut Senekowitsch

HOLLAND

Goalkeepers	1	Piet Schrijvers	*Ajax*
	8	Jan Jongbloed	*Roda JC*
	19	Wim Doesburg	*Sparta*
Defenders	3	Dirk Schoenaker	*Ajax*
	4	Adrie Van Kraaij	*PSV Eindhoven*
	5	Ruud Krol	*Ajax*
	7	Piet Wildschut	*FC Twente*
	17	Wim Rijsbergen	*Feyenoord*
	20	Wim Suurbier	*Schalke 04*
	22	Erny Brandts	*PSV Eindhoven*
Midfield	2	Jan Poortvliet	*PSV Eindhoven*
	6	Wim Jansen	*Feyenoord*
	9	Arie Haan	*Anderlecht*
	11	Willy Van de Kerkhof	*PSV Eindhoven*
	13	Johan Neeskens	*Barcelona*
	14	Jan Boskamp	*RWDM*
	15	Hugo Hovekamp	*AZ '67*
Forwards	10	Rene Van der Kerkhof	*PSV Eindhoven*
	12	Rob Rensenbrink	*Anderlecht*
	16	Johnny Rep	*Bastia*
	18	Dirk Nanninga	*Roda JC*
	21	Henricus Lubse	*PSV Eindhoven*

Manager Ernst Happel

BRAZIL

Goalkeepers	1	Emerson Leao	*Palmeiras*
	12	Carlos Roberto Galo	*Ponte Preta*
	22	Waldir Peres	*Sao Paolo*
Defenders	2	Antonio Dias dos Santos	*Flamengo*
	3	Jose Oscar Bernardi	*Ponte Preta*
	4	Joao Justino Amaral dos Santos	*Corinthians*
	6	Edinho Nazareth Filho	*Fluminense*
	13	Manoel de Mattos Cabral	*Cruziero*
	14	Abel Carlos da Silva Braga	*Vasco da Gama*
	15	Jose Fernando Polozi	*Ponte Preta*
	16	Jose Rodrigues Neto	*Botafogo*
Midfield	5	Antonio Carlos Cerezo	*Atletico*
	10	Roberto Rivelino	*Fluminense*
	11	Dirceu Jose Guimaraes	*Vasco da Gama*
	17	Joao Batista da Silva	*Internacional*
	21	(Chicao) Francisco Avanzi	*Sao Paolo*
Forwards	7	Jose Sergio Presti	*Sao Paolo*
	8	(Zico) Arthur Antunes Coimbra	*Flamengo*
	9	Jose Reinaldo de Lima	*Atletico*
	18	Gilberto Alves	*Botafogo*
	19	Jorge Pinto Mendonca	*Botafogo*
	20	Carlos Roberto de Oliveira	*Vasco da Gama*

Manager Claudio Coutinho

HUNGARY

Goalkeepers	1	Sandor Gujdar	*Bp Honved*
	21	Ferenc Meszaros	*Bp Vasas*
	22	Laszlo Kovacs	*Videoton*
Defenders	2	Peter Torok	*Bp Vasas*
	3	Istvan Kocsis	*Bp Honved*
	4	Jozsef Toth	*Ujpest Dozsa*
	6	Zoltan Kereki	*Szombathelyl Haladas*
	12	Gyozo Martos	*FTC*
	14	Laszlo Balint	*FTC*
	15	Tibor Rab	*FTC*
Midfield	5	Sandor Zombori	*Bp Vasas*
	8	Tibor Nyilasi	*FTC*
	10	Sandor Pinter	*Bp Honved*
	13	Karoly Csapo	*Tatabanya*
	16	Istvan Halasz	*Tatabanya*
	19	Andras Toth	*Ujpest Dozsa*
Forwards	7	Laszlo Fazekas	*Ujpest Dozsa*
	9	Andras Torocsik	*Ujpest Dozsa*
	11	Bela Varady	*Bp Vasas*
	17	Laszlo Pusztai	*FTC*
	18	Laszlo Nagy	*Ujpest Dozsa*
	20	Ferenc Fulop	*MTK VM*

Manager Lajos Baroti

IRAN

alkeepers	1	Nasser Hejazi	*Shahbaz*
	12	Bahram Movedat	*Sepahan*
	22	Mohammad Karbekandl	*Zobe Ahan*
Defenders	5	Javad Allahvardi	*Persepolis*
	11	Ali Reza Ghashghaian	*Bargh*
	14	Hassan Nazari	*Tadj*
	15	Adranik Eskandarjan	*Tadj*
	19	Ali Shjaee	*Sepahan*
	20	Nasrollah Abdollahi	*Shahbaz*
	21	Hossein Kazerani	*Pass*
Midfield	2	Iraj Danalfar	*Tadj*
	3	Bektash Farabi	*Rah Ahan*
	6	Hassan Naibagha	*Homa*
	7	Ali Parvin	*Persepolis*
	8	Ebrahim Ghasimpour	*Shahbaz*
	9	Mohammad Sadeghi	*Pass*
Forwards	4	Majeed Bishkar	*Rastakhiz*
	10	Hassan Rowshan	*Tadj*
	13	Hamid-Majd Taymouri	*Shahbaz*
	16	Nasser Nouraii	*Homa*
	17	Ghafour Jahani	*Malavan*
	18	Hossein Faraki	*Pass*

Manager Heshmat Mohajerani

PERU

Goalkeepers	1	Ottorino Sartor	*CNI*
	13	Juan Caceres	*Alianza Lima*
	21	Ramon Quiroga	*S Cristal*
Defenders	3	Rodolfo Manzo	*D Municipal*
	4	Hector Chumpitaz	*S Cristal*
	5	Toribio Diaz	*S Cristal*
	9	Percy Rojas	*S Cristal*
	14	Jose Navarro	*S Cristal*
	15	German Leguia	*D Municipal*
Midfield	2	Jaime Duarte	*Alianza Lima*
	6	Jose Velasquez	*Alianza Lima*
	10	Teofilo Cubillas	*Alianza Lima*
	16	Raul Gorriti	*S Cristal*
	17	Alfredo Quesada	*S Cristal*
	18	Ernesto Labarthe	*Sport Boys*
Forwards	7	Juan Munante	*Union de Mexico*
	8	Cesar Cueto	*Alianza Lima*
	11	Juan Oblitas	*S Cristal*
	12	Roberto Mosquera	*S Cristal*
	19	Guillermo La Rosa	*Alianza Lima*
	20	Hugo Sotil	*Alianza Lima*
	22	Roberto Rojas	*Alianza Lima*

Manager Marcos Calderon

ITALY

alkeepers	1	Dino Zoff	*Juventus*
	12	Paolo Conti	*Roma*
	22	Ivano Bordon	*Inter*
Defenders	2	Mauro Bellugi	*Bologna*
	3	Antonio Cabrini	*Juventus*
	4	Antonello Cuccureddu	*Juventus*
	5	Claudio Gentile	*Juventus*
	6	Aldo Maldera	*Juventus*
	7	Lionello Manfredonia	*Lazio*
	8	Gaetano Scirea	*Juventus*
	14	Marco Tardelli	*Juventus*
Midfield	9	Giancarlo Antognoni	*Fiorentina*
	10	Romeo Benetti	*Juventus*
	11	Eraldo Pecci	*Torino*
	13	Patrizio Sala	*Torino*
	15	Renato Zaccarelli	*Torino*
	16	Franco Causio	*Juventus*
Forwards	17	Claudio Sala	*Torino*
	18	Roberto Bettega	*Juventus*
	19	Francesco Graziani	*Torino*
	20	Paolino Pulici	*Torino*
	21	Paolo Rossi	*Lanerossi Vicenza*

Manager Enzo Bearzot

POLAND

Goalkeepers	1	Jan Tomaszewski	*LKS Lodz*
	21	Zygmunt Kukla	*Stal Mielec*
	22	Zdzislaw Kostrzewa	*Zaglebie Sosnowiec*
Defenders	3	Henryk Maculewicz	*Wisla Krakow*
	4	Antoni Szymanowski	*Wisla Krakow*
	6	Jerzy Gorgon	*Gomik Zabrze*
	9	Wladislaw Zmuda	*Slask Wrclaw*
	10	Wojciech Rudy	*Zaglebie Sosnowiec*
	14	Miroslaw Justek	*Lech Poznan*
Midfield	5	Adam Nawalka	*Wisla Krakow*
	8	Henryk Kasperczak	*Stal Mielec*
	11	Bohdan Masztaler	*LKS Lodz*
	12	Kazimierz Deyna	*Legia Warszawa*
	13	Janusz Kupcewicz	*Arka Gdynia*
	18	Zbigniew Boniek	*Widzew Lodz*
	20	Roman Wojcicki	*Odra Opole*
Forwards	2	Wlodzimierz Mazur	*Zaglebie Sosnowiec*
	7	Andrzej Iwan	*Wisla Krakow*
	15	Marek Kusto	*Legia Warszawa*
	16	Grzegorz Lato	*Stal Mielec*
	17	Andrzej Szarmach	*Stal Mielec*
	19	Wlodzimierz Lubanski	*Lokeren Belgia*

Manager Jacek Gmoch

MEXICO

alkeepers	1	Jose Pilar-Reyes	*U. de Nuevo Leon*
	22	Pedro Soto	*America*
Defenders	2	Manuel Najera	*U. de Guadalajara*
	3	Alfredo Tena	*America*
	4	Eduardo Ramos	*Guadalajara*
	5	Arturo Vasquez-Ayala	*UNAM*
	12	Jesus Martinez	*America*
	13	Rigoberto Cisneros	*Toluca*
	14	Carlos Gomez	*Leon*
	15	Ignacio Flores	*Cruz Azul*
Midfield	6	Guillermo Mendizabal	*Cruz Azul*
	7	Antonio de la Torre	*America*
	8	Enrique Lopez Zarza	*UNAM*
	16	Javier Cardenas	*Toluca*
	17	Leonardo Cuellar	*UNAM*
	18	Gerardo Lugo	*Atlante*
Forwards	9	Victor Rangel	*Guadalajara*
	10	Cristobal Ortega	*America*
	11	Hugo Sanchez	*UNAM*
	19	Hugo Rodrigues	*Laguna*
	20	Mario Medina	*Toluca*
	21	Raul Isiordia	*Atletico Espanol*

Manager Jose Antonio Roca

SCOTLAND

Goalkeepers	1	Alan Rough	*Partick Thistle*
	12	Jim Blyth	*Coventry City*
	20	Bobby Clark	*Aberdeen*
Defenders	2	Sandy Jardine	*Rangers*
	3	Willie Donachie	*Manchester City*
	4	Martin Buchan	*Manchester United*
	5	Gordon McQueen	*Manchester United*
	13	Stuart Kennedy	*Aberdeen*
	14	Tom Forsyth	*Rangers*
	22	Kenny Burns	*Nottingham Forest*
Midfield	6	Bruce Riocl.	*Derby County*
	7	Don Masson	*Derby County*
	10	Asa Hartford	*Manchester City*
	15	Archie Gemmill	*Nottingham Forest*
	16	Lou Macari	*Manchester United*
	18	Graeme Souness	*Liverpool*
Forwards	8	Kenny Dalglish	*Liverpool*
	9	Joe Jordan	*Manchester United*
	11	Willie Johnston	*West Bromwich Albion*
	13	Derek Johnstone	*Rangers*
	19	John Robertson	*Nottingham Forest*
	21	Joe Harper	*Aberdeen*

Manager Ally MacLeod

SPAIN		
Goalkeepers	13 Miguel Angel Gonzalez	*Real Madrid*
	1 Luis Arconada	*Real Sociedad*
	22 Francisco Gonzalez	*RCD Espanol*
Defenders	5 Miguel Bernardo	*Barcelona*
	6 Antonio Biosca	*Real Betis Balompie*
	2 Jesus Antonio de la Cruz	*Barcelona*
	16 Antonio Olmo	*Barcelona*
	17 Marcelino Perez	*Atletico Madrid*
	18 Jose Martinez Pirri	*Real Madrid*
	21 Isidoro San Jose	*Real Madrid*
Midfield	3 Francisco Javier Alvarez	*Real Sporting*
	4 Juan Manuel Asensi	*Barcelona*
	11 Julio Cardenosa	*Real Betis Balompie*
	12 Antonio Guzman	*AD Roya Vallecano*
	14 Eugenio Leal	*Atletico Madrid*
Forwards	7 Daniel Ruiz-Bazan	*Athletic Club*
	8 Juan(ito) Gomez	*Real Madrid*
	9 (Quini) Enrique Castro	*Real Sporting*
	10 (Santillana) Carlos Alonso	*Real Madrid*
	15 (Maranon) Rafael Carlos Perez	*RCD Espanol*
	19 Carlos Rexach	*Barcelona*
	20 Ruben Andres Cano	*Atletico Madrid*
Manager	Ladislao Kubala	

TUNISIA		
Goalkeepers	1 Sadak Sassi	*Club Africain*
	21 Lamine Ben Aziza	*ES Sahel*
	22 Moktah Naili	*Club Africain*
Defenders	2 Moktah Dhouib	*CS Sfaxien*
	3 Ali Kaabi	*CO Transports*
	4 Khaled Gasmi	*CA Bizertin*
	5 Mohsen dit Jendoubi Labidi	*Stade Tun*
	14 Slah Karoui	*ES Sahel*
	17 Ridha Ellouz	*SR Sports*
	18 Chebli Kamel	*Club Africain*
	20 Amar Jebali	*AS Marsa*
Midfield	6 Nejib Gommidh	*Club Africain*
	8 Mohamed Ben Rehaiem	*CS Sfaxien*
	10 Dhiab Tarek	*ES Tunis*
	12 Khemais Labidi	*JS Kairouanaise*
	15 Mohamed Ali Ben Moussa	*Club Africai*
Forwards	7 Lahzami Temime	*ES Tunis*
	9 Mohamed Ali Akid	*CS Sfaxien*
	13 Mohamed Nejib Liman	*Stade Tunisien*
	16 Ohman Chehaibi	*JS Kairouanaise*
	19 Moktah Hasni	*Louivière (Belgium)*
	21 Raouf Ben Aziza	*ES Sahel*
Manager	Majid Chetali	

SWEDEN		
Goalkeepers	1 Ronnie Hellström	*1 FC Kaiserslautern*
	12 Göran Hagberg	*Osters IF*
	17 Jan Möller	*Malmö FF*
Defenders	2 Hasse Borg	*Eintracht Braunschweig*
	3 Roy Andersson	*Malmö FF*
	4 Björn Nordqvist	*IFK Göteborg*
	5 Ingemar Erlandsson	*Malmö FF*
	13 Magnus Andersson	*Malmö FF*
	14 Ronald Aman	*Orebro SK*
	19 Kent Karlsson	*IFK Eskilstuna*
	20 Roland Andersson	*Malmö FF*
Midfield	6 Staffen Tapper	*Malmö FF*
	7 Anders Linderoth	*Olympique Marseille*
	8 Bo Larsson	*Malmö FF*
	9 Lennart Larsson	*Shalke 04*
	16 Conny Torstensson	*FC Zürich*
	18 Olle Nordin	*IFK Göteborg*
Forwards	10 Thomas Sjoberg	*Malmö FF*
	11 Benny Wendt	*1 FC Kaiserslautern*
	15 Torbjörn Nilsson	*IFK Göteborg*
	21 Sanny Aslund	*ALK*
	22 Ralf Edström	*IFK Göteborg*
Manager	Georg Ericsson	

WEST GERMANY		
Goalkeepers	1 Sepp Maier	*Bayern München*
	21 Rudi Kargus	*Hamburger SV*
	22 Dieter Burdenski	*Werder Bremen*
Defenders	2 Berti Vogts	*Mönchengladbach*
	3 Bernard Dietz	*MSV Duisburg*
	4 Rolf Rüssmann	*Schalke 04*
	5 Manfred Kaltz	*Hamburger SV*
	8 Herbert Zimmerman	*1 FC Köln*
	12 Georg Schwarzenbeck	*Bayern München*
	13 Harald Konopka	*1 FC Köln*
Midfield	6 Rainer Bonhof	*Mönchengladbach*
	10 Heinz Flohe	*1 FC Köln*
	15 Erich Beer	*Hertha BSC*
	16 Bernd Cullmann	*1 FC Köln*
	17 Bernd Holzenbein	*Eintracht Frankfurt*
	18 Gerd Zewe	*Fortuna Düsseldorf*
	20 Hans Müller	*VfB Stuttgart*
Forwards	7 Rüdiger Abramczik	*Schalke 04*
	9 Klaus Fischer	*Schalke 04*
	11 Karl-Heinz Rummenigge	*Bayern Münch*
	14 Dieter Müller	*1 FC Köln*
	19 Ronald Worm	*MSV Duisberg*
Manager	Helmut Schön	

OFFICIALS

Referees and/or linesmen

Angel Coerezza	*Argentina*	Sergio Gonella	*Italy*	Anatoli Ivanov	*USSR*
Erich Linemayr	*Austria*	Alfonso Archundia	*Mexico*	Clive Thomas	*Wales*
Francis Rion	*Belgium*	Charles Corvér	*Netherlands*	Dusan Maksimovic	*Yugoslavia*
Arnaldo Coelho	*Brazil*	Cesar Orozco	*Peru*		
Werner Winsemann	*Canada*	Alojzy Jarguz	*Poland*	**Linesmen only**	
Juan Silvagno	*Chile*	Antonio Jose da Silva Garrido	*Portugal*	Miguel Comesana	*Argentina*
Patrick Partridge	*England*	Nicolai Rainea	*Romania*	Arturo Ithurralde	*Argentina*
Gebreyesus Tesfaye	*Ethiopia*	John Gordon	*Scotland*	Luis Pestarino	*Argentina*
Robert Wurtz	*France*	Youssou N'Diaye	*Senegal*		
Adolf Prokop	*East German*	Angel Franco Martinez	*Spain*	**Reserves**	
Ferdinand Biwersi	*West German*	Ulf Eriksson	*Sweden*	Franz Woehrer	*Austria*
Karoly Palotai	*Hungary*	Jean Dubach	*Switzerland*	Alfred Delcourt	*Belgium*
Jafar Namdar	*Iran*	Farouk Bouzo	*Syria*	Romualdo Arppi Filho	*Brazil*
Abraham Klein	*Israel*	Hedi Seoudi	*Tunisia*	Michel Kitabdjian	*France*
		Ramon Barreto Ruiz	*Uruguay*	Heinz Aldinger	*West Germany*
				Alberto Michelotti	*Italy*